Marblehead's PYGMALION

FINDING THE REAL *Agnes Surriage*

F. MARSHALL BAUER

Charleston London

THE
History
PRESS

Published by The History Press
Charleston, SC 29403
www.historypress.net

First published 2010

Manufactured in the United States

ISBN 978.1.60949.068.3

Library of Congress Cataloging-in-Publication Data
Bauer, F. Marshall.
Marblehead's Pygmalion : finding the real Agnes Surriage / F. Marshall Bauer.
p. cm.
Includes bibliographical references.
ISBN 978-1-60949-068-3
1. Surriage, Agnes, 1726-1783. 2. Surriage, Agnes, 1726-1783--Legends. 3. Marblehead
(Mass.)--Biography. 4. Women--Massachusetts--Marblehead--Biography. 5. Social classes--
Massachusetts--Marblehead--History--18th century. 6. Marblehead (Mass.)--Social life and
customs--18th century. 7. Mistresses--Massachusetts--Hopkinton--Biography. 8. Surriage,
Agnes 1726-1783--Marriage. 9. Frankland, Charles Henry, Sir, 1716-1768. 10. Chichester
(England)--Biography. I. Title.
F74.M3B2 2010
974.4'02092--dc22
[B]
2010042771

For Janie and Terri

Contents

CONTENTS

Foreword

M arshall Bauer has been fascinated by the legend of Agnes Surriage for as long as I have known him. This fascination has led him to extensive research and reflection. The result is *Marblehead's Pygmalion: Finding the Real Agnes Surriage*.

The legend of Agnes Surriage and Sir Harry Frankland, Marblehead's Cinderella and her Prince Charming, is well known. In this book, the story is not just retold but reinterpreted. The author has researched, examined and turned the story inside out searching for historical context and documentation. Bauer has worked to confirm, support, understand and explain the well-known tale.

His investigative approach to the romanticized true story is well done, as are his efforts to add fact to fiction. Bauer's research finds interesting connections between reality and myth. He is a historical detective, and the reader follows him to both interesting conclusions and frustrating conundrums. Each answered question leads to another puzzle, as well as a deeper layer of understanding

It is both interesting and informative to follow Agnes Surriage and Harry Frankland's story through Marshall Bauer's research. It is admirable that Bauer's interest and determination have led to real facts and insights. *Marblehead's Pygmalion* is a valuable addition to both legend and fact of life in colonial America.

Pam Peterson, Director, Marblehead Museum and Historical Society

Acknowledgements

Every author of nonfiction history should have a woman like Libby Franck as a friend. A professional storyteller, Libby is a library science graduate of Wellesley and Simmons Colleges. She has a keen sense of history as drama and an ability to spot significant detail. Over the past ten years, she has helped me dig historical dust out of the nooks and crannies of old books, newspapers and museum documents.

The influence and support of a skilled journalist—my pal, literary sounding board and valued colleague Francie King—recharged my creative batteries during those fearsome moments of writer's block.

Pam Peterson and Karen Mac Innis, of the Marblehead Museum and Historical Society, have been silent partners to virtually every researcher, author and actor involved in a project dealing with Marblehead history. Their help with Ashley Bowen's journal and the Second Church records, in addition to a willingness to donate their valuable time and knowledge of eighteenth-century Marblehead, provided invaluable guidance in my search for the truth.

From its vast collection of documents, the Massachusetts Historical Society supplied a wealth of material. I am especially indebted to Elaine Grublin, reference librarian, for the rare opportunity to examine and photograph the original copy of Sir Charles Henry Frankland's diary.

Many organizations in England have been instrumental in helping me reconstruct Agnes's life: the British Library, the Yorkshire Archaeological Society, the Nottinghamshire Archives, the British Museum and the

Chichester City Council. I am particularly grateful to Simon Martin, director of Pallent House Gallery in Chichester, for his photograph of the only known Agnes Surriage portrait, and to Anne Scicluna, Chichester historian, for her photograph of Lady Frankland's house.

The Other Woman

Agnes Surriage has been a part of my daily life since November 1, 1973, when my late wife, Jane, and I moved from Pennsylvania to our new home at the site where the Fountain Inn stood in 1741. Every time I make the right-hand turn from Orne Street onto Fountain Inn Lane, I pass a huge historical marker that encapsulates—in just forty-three words—two fascinating and eventful lives lived over a combined span of sixty-seven years:

> *Agnes Surriage Well*
> *Belonging to the Fountain Inn,*
> *Where Sir Harry Frankland,*
> *Collector of the Port of Boston,*
> *While supervising the erection*
> *Of Fort Sewall met Agnes,*
> *A poor fisherman's daughter who*
> *Later became Lady Frankland*
> *And returned with her husband to England.*

My southwest windows face the Agnes Surriage well, where Charles Henry Frankland is said to have first laid eyes on the adolescent barmaid. I climb down to the water's edge on the same granite boulders she trod in her bare feet. Her story is inescapable. I literally live at its wellspring.

Legends have always awakened my skepticism. They are like the parlor game in which "A" whispers a story in the ear of "B," who then passes it down the line. By the time it gets to "G," the original is distorted beyond recognition. Substitute generations for alphabetized people and you have the evolution of a legend. According to Pam Peterson, director of the Marblehead Museum and Historical Society, "Myths and legends can be and are edited all the time."[1]

For some reason, I was immediately annoyed by the sign's truncated version of the Agnes Surriage legend. The limitations of space are understandable, but it opened huge gaps. Under what conditions would a highborn Englishman meet a dirt-poor fisherman's daughter? Why would he cross the rigid class barriers of the eighteenth century to marry her? Exactly what happened between "met Agnes" and "returned with her husband to England"?

My research instincts kicked in. I read all of the Agnes Surriage poems, novels and magazine articles I could get my hands on. There have been plenty: "Agnes," Oliver Wendell Holmes's 1861 epic poem; a biography, *Sir Charles Henry Frankland, Baronet*, by Elias Nason in 1865; the 1910 romance novel *Agnes Surriage*, by Edwin Lassetter Byner; *Lady Good-for-Nothing*, a fictional romance also penned in 1910, by Arthur T. Quiller-Couch; and *Yankee Cinderella*, published in 1996. Her story has been repeated over and over in magazines and countless anthologies of New England lore.

Without exception, everything I found romanticized the legend, highlighting its fairy tale similarity. As a result, readers have been left with an image of Lady Frankland as a metaphor for Cinderella: a perpetually young and beautiful sixteen-year-old serving girl, ragtag and barefoot.

It was time for a new look at the old story. My goal was to deconstruct the legend, find the real Lady Frankland and interpret her world for a generation that has experienced a sexual revolution and the ascendancy of feminism.

I became an investigative reporter with one foot in the past and the other in the present. As if searching for some essence of Agnes's being, I walked through North Boston and Hopkinton; exchanged lengthy correspondence with librarians and archivists in Yorkshire, Chichester and Nottingham; and spent hours downloading eighteenth-century documents from the Internet. My 25 years of research have been accompanied by continuous study of Harry Frankland's personal journal, first on microfilm at the Massachusetts Historical Society; then in Marblehead, with a copy that the society generously sent to the Abbot Library; and finally, through the pages of the 255-year-old original leather-bound volume.

The more I learned about Agnes, the tighter her grip became on me and the more I felt that the existing literature had done her a gross injustice.

You will not find a typical historical biography here. It is more like a voiceover narrative of my journey into the lives of Agnes and Harry. The facts are often accompanied by speculation and conjecture based on my discoveries. I believe these interpretations are a legitimate part of the story.

Searching for Agnes has been an adventure prompted by a passion for history combined with a deep respect for the truth. I believe that study of the past is more about people and the emotions they felt than places, dates and events. My guiding principles have been the elements of historical thinking enunciated by Jacquelyn Hall, Julia Cherry Spruill Professor and Director, Southern Oral History Program, University of North Carolina at Chapel Hill:

> *Analyzing Evidence,*
> *Weighing conflicting Interpretations,*
> *Discerning Causality,*
> *Developing Arguments, and*
> *Contextualizing the present in the light of the past.*

I've discovered a tale of money, lust and vindication; there are no magic pumpkins, no glass slippers, no wicked stepmother or stepsisters and absolutely no Prince Charming. If there is a metaphor here, it is Pygmalion—certainly not Cinderella.

As I worked, I could not help noticing how toxic the Cinderella fable has become. Every time someone paraphrases it, he unwittingly reinforces a medieval put-down of women. Prince Charming, although an ardent suitor, is always regal, superior—the master. He is never partner or friend. Cinderella is eternally grateful, never equal.

Abigail Adams said it all in a letter to John in 1776 while he was attending the Continental Congress: "That your sex are naturally tyrannical is a truth so thoroughly established as to admit of no dispute, but such of you as wish to be happy willingly give up the harsh title of master for the more tender and endearing one of friend."[2]

This work is one man's brotherly salute to all those women who quietly endured centuries of marginalization with dignity and self-respect—the ones who never accepted the role of supplicant.

Join my search for the real Agnes Surriage. I hope you will enjoy the process of extracting a fine woman from the quagmire of fairy tale fiction that has burdened her memory for over a century and a half.

November 1, 1755

It is a brilliant Saturday morning, warm for late autumn. Under a clear sky, the ships at anchor in the Tangus River present a gently rocking forest of masts and rigging.

Today, the Catholic Church celebrates All Saints' Day, one of the holiest observances in the Christian year, honoring all saints, "known and unknown, past, present, and future." Lisbon's cathedrals are packed with the faithful; its streets are jammed with others on their way to and from worship.

A chaise, driven by a liveried groom riding postillion on the left horse of a pair, weaves through the milling crowds. Within, Sir Charles Henry Frankland sits erect, viewing the Catholic masses in the manner of an affluent Anglican.

The baronet has everything going for him. Using his connections, he can go just about anywhere in the world and do almost anything that catches his fancy. At present, he and Lady Agnes Frankland are renting a house in the wealthy British community, surrounded by virtually every creature comfort known to man.

The English residents of eighteenth-century Lisbon—most of whom work in the "British factory," or trading house—are awash in sensual pleasure. They immerse themselves in the most fashionable art and music, swill the world's best wines, gorge themselves with rich food and gleefully indulge in elegant depravity.

As Frankland's chaise enters a narrow lane at about 9:30 a.m., there is a faint rumbling sound, which increases rapidly. The vehicle bounces. Sir

Harry looks up, cursing his driver for hitting a stone in the road. With a sickening twist, the ground buckles and rolls like waves in the sea. Great cracks appear in the street. Houses begin to sway like willows in a whirlwind. Sir Harry's chaise rocks violently from side to side. Instinctively, he jumps to the ground as a building collapses on his groom and horses, killing them. From every direction, glass, wood, bricks and chunks of plaster fly at him, slamming into his body and throwing him to the heaving ground.

Covered by debris and convinced he is a dead man, Harry does not hear the rolling thunder and agonized screams that only a catastrophic earthquake can produce.

Sir Charles Henry Frankland is buried alive.

Where I Started

The Accepted Legend

Our search for Agnes begins with a condensed version of her legend. Here are the basic elements as they have been handed down by word of mouth and fictionalized in print.

In the autumn of 1742, Charles Henry Frankland, collector of the Port of Boston, arrived in Marblehead to supervise reconstruction of the town's fort. As Frankland's carriage, complete with King's seal and uniformed livery, drew up to the Fountain Inn, Agnes Surriage, the sixteen-year-old serving girl, was scrubbing the steps. When he approached her to ask the whereabouts of Innkeeper Nathaniel Bartlett, Agnes's long dark hair, fair skin and natural beauty immediately captivated the collector. Noticing that she was barefoot, Frankland gave the maid a gold coin "to buy yourself a good pair of shoes."

On his return, he noticed Agnes still barefoot. When asked why she hadn't bought shoes, she answered, "Sor, oi did. And savin' them oi am tuh wear tuh meetin a' Sonday." In the ensuing months, Frankland found reason to revisit Marblehead frequently.

It was not long before Frankland had convinced her mother and father, along with her minister, Edward Holyoke, that Agnes should become his ward so that he could take her to Boston, where he would pay for her education.

He boarded her with a family in Boston and enrolled her in Peter Pelham's school near the customhouse. Agnes applied herself to the lessons. Over the next several years, the poor serving girl thrived and blossomed into a beautiful and talented young woman.

Orne Street on the way to the Fountain Inn. *Courtesy of the Marblehead Museum and Historical Society.*

Frankland became her constant companion. Finally, unable to hide their love for each other, they began living together in the collector's North End home without the formality of marriage. A gathering storm of gossip surrounded the couple. Agnes fell from gentle condescension to abject scorn in the eyes of Boston society.

The collector inherited the baronetcy in 1746, when his uncle died. He was now Sir Charles Henry Frankland. With this change in his station, Agnes faced a new onslaught of outrage and prejudice as the lowborn mistress of a titled Englishman. It began to affect her health.

In 1751, Sir Harry bought a huge tract of land in Hopkinton, thirty miles northwest of Boston. There he built a sumptuous estate, with many of the building materials imported from England. He also acquired rare flowering plants and fruit trees from all over the world. Here, the two lovers would be safe from the gossip and innuendos of Boston society. Harry's natural son, Henry Cromwell, who was about ten years old, joined them.

Three years later, a pressing family matter required Sir Harry's return to England. Agnes accompanied him. Once again, she met a solid wall of ostracism at the hands of the Frankland family and the Nottingham gentry. When his business was completed, Sir Harry and Agnes toured the Continent, finally settling in Lisbon, where there was a substantial community of English expatriates.

On the morning of November 1, 1755, Sir Charles Henry Frankland was riding in his chaise with another woman when the great All Saints' Day earthquake struck Lisbon. A building fell on his carriage, instantly killing horses, groom and his companion, who, in her agony, bit through the sleeve of Sir Harry's coat, tearing the flesh of his arm. Frankland was not killed but buried alive.

In his living tomb, Harry sought divine mercy for his life of indolence, vowing that if spared, he would live differently. He promised that his first act would be marrying Agnes so that they no longer lived in sin. Meanwhile, Agnes had dashed from their residence in panic. She knew the route Sir Harry would have taken, so she ran in search of him. Coming upon a pile of timber and plaster, she miraculously heard his voice crying for help. Agnes began tearing at the rubble with her bare hands and then ripping the sliver buckles from her shoes; she offered them to men passing by to help her dig.

Frankland emerged a new man. He took Agnes to the nearest Catholic priest and married her. Later, on the boat that would begin their journey back to Nottingham, a Church of England minister married the couple a second time.

On their return, Agnes was welcomed into the Frankland family as a heroine.

And they lived happily ever after.

PART I
Money

CHAPTER 1

Ed Surriage's Daughter

I began my search with an unscholarly but important question: what did my mystery woman look like?

Her "ringlets of raven hair" (Nason), "full black eyes instinct with passion" (Byner) and "angel's shape and air" (Holmes) are all remnants of interviews with fourth-generation Hopkinton servants and nineteenth-century Surriage relatives. At best, they consist of romanticized mental images of a stereotypical Cinderella embellished through more than one hundred years of passing from one generation to another.

A portrait of Agnes done when she was in her fifties gave me a little more accurate indication. It shows a double chin and slight under bite. However, she still looks perky right down to the dimple in her chin. There is an unmistakable twinkle in her eye and a dainty button nose. It is not difficult to imagine the tavern maid who caught Charles Henry Frankland's attention.

On her mother's side, Agnes came from sturdy English stock. Her great-grandfather, blacksmith John Brown, emigrated from Bristol, England, to Pemaquid in 1622.[3] Today, Pemaquid is in Maine, but in the colonial period the territory was considered part of Massachusetts.

John Brown's daughter Elizabeth married Richard Pierce (I).
Richard Pierce (I)   Elizabeth Brown
Their son, Richard Pierce (II), was the father of Mary Pierce, who married Edward Surriage.
Richard Pierce (II)   Mary (surname unknown)

Dame Agnes Frankland,
1783, by John Raphael
Smith (1752–1812).
Pastel on paper courtesy
of Pallant House Gallery,
Chichester, UK.

Edward Surriage   Mary Pierce
                         Agnes Surriage

John Brown was probably the first permanent settler of Maine.[4] Records show that he was a blacksmith living in Pemaquid, now known as Bristol, prior to 1639. He is listed as a "fur trader" in 1625, when he is said to have bought territory including today's Damariscotta and Bristol from the Indians. This purchase would become known as the "Brown Tract." His landholdings further expanded in 1639 as he and Edward Bateman acquired "all lands between the Sagadahoc and Sheepscot Rivers."

During the late seventeenth and early eighteenth centuries, Agnes's ancestors were fishermen and Indian traders living in Muscongus near Pemaquid. To the south, a fishing station that would become Marblehead was growing on a peninsula twenty miles north of Boston. The Browns and Pierces frequently shifted between these two locations to escape Indian uprisings. Maine records from 1717 show that her grandfather, Richard Pierce, was "a coaster fisherman of Marblehead, age 70." By 1718, he was back in Muscongus.

These erratic peregrinations and the absence of early records made it difficult to determine exactly where and when Mary Pierce was born.

Little is known of Edward Surriage, except that he "owned the covenant May 15, 1720" in the Second Congregational Church of Marblehead.[5] Mary Surriage's first child, Edward, was baptized July 5, 1719.[6] Considering the strict fornication laws of the time, and the fact that Mary's neighbors would have been counting months, it's safe to assume she was married by then.

On April 17, 1726, Edward Holyoke, minister of Marblehead's second church, recorded that he baptized "Agnis [sic] Surriage infant of Edward and Mary Surriage."[7]

The Julian calendar in use at the time confirms that it was Sunday. Mary would most likely have attended the baptism alone because Ed was at sea fishing. Carrying the baby wrapped in a blanket, she would have been wearing her heaviest cloak, for the weather was still cold in April. (North America had been in the midst of a mini ice age since 1650.) Like a six-year-old in any time frame, the boy Edward Surriage would have been running and skipping ahead of his mother, while little Mary Surriage, a toddler of four, clung to the hem of her mother's garment. Uncle John Pierce, baker and church deacon, and his wife could have been included in the family procession as they joined the stream of worshipers flowing in and around the empty stalls of Market Square, passing the "gaol and cage"[8] on their way to the dirt road called "The Way to the New Meeting House."

Agnes would be the fourth of Ed and Mary Surriage's eight children listed in Second Church records.[9] She was born into the hardscrabble existence of a Marblehead fisherman's family. In the seventeenth century, fishing ships were small—seldom more than twenty feet. Waves tossed these tiny vessels like walnut shells bobbing in the rush of a spring flood, while fishermen, struggling to keep from falling overboard, dropped hand lines over the side. Their job was both tiring and hazardous. Cod feed near the bottom, which meant fighting thirty- to sixty-pound fish through well over one hundred feet of water from dawn to nightfall.

Shortly before Agnes was born, the fishing schooner became the vessel of choice. It was more rugged, extending the fleet's range farther off shore through the stormy North Atlantic waters to the Grand Banks. With the safety of crew members hanging over the rail in mind, Marblehead shipwrights evolved a unique design featuring a raised deck from the schooner's stern to the mainmast. Because it looked like a shoe floating upside down in the water, this innovation became known as the "heel tapper."

Ed Surriage's work was backbreaking and dangerous. Nor was it limited to grown men—boys from eight to twelve would go to sea. Their pay was based on the number of fish they brought aboard, identified by a notch cut in the tail. It was not long before their older shipmates coined the term "cuttails."

The fleet left Marblehead in February, not to return until mid-September. Often, they would take one more "fare" during late fall and early winter.

Marblehead fishermen's wives were known for their independent, and sometimes feisty, behavior—a persona that emerged early in the town's history and was embellished over time. Many of the poor Jersey and Guernsey fishermen who settled this peninsula couldn't afford to bring their wives with them. As a result, there was a severe shortage of women in Marblehead during the seventeenth century. This resulted in aggressive behavior on the part of both sexes. As Christine Leigh Heyrman reports in her comprehensive study of early Marblehead, the "intense competition for the companionship of the community's women" led to frequent abusive advances by men, while wives found themselves with a choice of mates, often dumping older, balding husbands for younger replacements.[10]

The dearth of women did nothing to enhance their position in the community.[11] It was an ironic twist on the law of supply and demand: instead of increasing in honor and esteem, women were considered property. They held the social status of indentured servants.

By the time Agnes was born, the number of men and women had become roughly equal. But the demands on fishermen's wives were still intense. Many were widowed by the natural occupational hazards of their husbands' work: storms, leaky ships and French pirates. Additionally, the Royal Navy, always in need of experienced seamen, had a habit of boarding fishing ships on the high seas and impressing crew members into the King's service.

Even those with living husbands faced challenges unique for women of the eighteenth century. Marblehead was virtually empty of men and boys from February to September. This resulted in a sharp cultural segregation of the sexes. While the men and older boys were off to the Grand Banks, their "codfish widows" stayed at home with daughters and small sons, tending the household and doing the physical work of men. Among other things, this included bargaining for cows, sheep, pigs and chickens and then slaughtering and cleaning them. It meant chopping wood and fixing leaky roofs, the backbreaking work of maintaining a vegetable garden and somehow finding the money for things that couldn't be made at home like soap and cloth, cooking utensils and tea.

Tending the fish flakes was a family affair. There were more than two hundred of these waist-level open frames for drying fish in town. Agnes and her siblings, along with their mother, were expected to help lash the saplings together, set up the flakes, split the cod and lay the carcasses out to dry.

As if the demands on them were not enough, fishermen's wives faced yet another serious challenge: loneliness combined with temptation. In February, just as the fleet left home for seven months, British merchant ships filled the harbor. Marblehead was overrun with English sailors. Between 1715 and 1735, Marblehead had nearly twice as many sexual misconduct cases as neighboring Salem. In Gloucester, most of the defendants in fornication cases were married couples whose child had arrived too soon after marriage, while nearly half of Marblehead's defendants were single women or wives.[12]

Searching the records of Marblehead's Second Church, I found twelve confessions of fornication made before the congregation by husbands and wives between 1720 and 1759. This example clearly reflects how much the intervening 290 years have changed attitudes toward premarital sex: "Some time in the spring of the year 1720 Nathan Ingalls & Mary his wife being each children of the church, both penitently and humbly made confession of the sin of fornication & had their child (who was begotten in fornication but born in lawful wedlock) baptized."

Violence was another serious issue confronting the codfish widows. Without men, they had no alternative but to protect their families alone. At this point, Marblehead was inhabited by a hard-drinking, raucous and often short-tempered citizenry. Drunken tavern brawls and fighting in the streets were common. Between 1716 and 1738, when Agnes was twelve, the number of townspeople indicted for violent crimes was more than double that of Salem, which had a much larger population.[13] This does not include the escapades of drunken sailors from foreign merchant ships. It would not be unusual for a codfish widow to find herself defending both her honor and her home with whatever was at hand, from a meat cleaver to the family musket.

Agnes grew up among women who were self-sufficient, proud and competent. These role models would have affected her view of women in general.

In 1730, when she was four, a major smallpox epidemic struck Marblehead. The unsanitary conditions under which they lived placed children in jeopardy virtually every day. Their mortality rate was high, ranging from 25 to 50 percent.[14] There is no record of the number of deaths in the plague, but according to historian Samuel Roads, it affected "rich and poor, old and young, the learned and the unlettered alike."[15] On December 21, 1730, the *New England Weekly Journal* reported: "We hear from Marblehead, that the Small-Pox begins to spread in that Town."

Simultaneously, conflict broke out over a new medical practice called "noculation." This was not twenty-first-century vaccination with the milder cowpox. A surgeon made a shallow incision in the arm of an uninfected patient, bandaging it with cloth containing fluid collected from the pustules of a person with smallpox. The inoculated patient contracted a mild case of pox but was immune for life. Many people, particularly the educated and affluent, believed it to be both effective and safe. Nine years before the outbreak in Marblehead, Zabdiel Boylston inoculated three hundred Bostonians. Only three died.

But many in this fishing village were skeptical. Their Calvinist roots dictated that God, and not man, should decide who lives and who dies. Preventing death from disease was interfering with His will.[16] Another objection to inoculation was its cost. The Town of Marblehead did not have enough money for a general inoculation. At the October 12, 1730 town meeting, the majority voted that unless everyone could be inoculated, the procedure would be banned. Rumors of people openly defiant of the ruling led to strong emotions, threats and mobs gathering at the homes of suspected offenders. Popular sympathy was with the crowd, however, and in the end, only four people were indicted for rioting and two for breach of the peace.[17]

By this time, the Surriage family consisted of Ed and Mary, plus Edward (eleven), Mary (eight), Josiah (five), Agnes and John (two). By December 1730, Mary was three months pregnant with Thomas, who would be born early the following June. The vulnerable ages of the Surriage children and Mary's condition suggested that they would be candidates for inclusion in Road's further statement that "many of the people in their terror fled from the town."[18]

Uncle John Pierce came to mind immediately. Unlike his fishermen father and brothers, John was a tradesman—a baker living in Marblehead—who would have been thirty-nine at the time of the epidemic. His roots were in Muscongus. He had deposed that he went there about 1722 to bring his father and family back.[19] Knowing the Pierce family's pattern of travel between Lincoln County and Marblehead, it is reasonable to consider that it would be only natural for John, the self-appointed patriarch, to pack up his sister's family and take them with his own to Pemaquid or Muscongus to wait for the end of the epidemic.

Whether he did is pure conjecture, but it is worth considering, since the life of the future Lady Frankland could well have hung in the balance.

CHAPTER 2

Oliver Cromwell's Great-Great-Grandson

In Victorian romance literature, Charles Henry Frankland leaps off the page bigger than life:

> *A young man of rank, wealth, talents—to say nothing of good looks, good breeding.*
> —*Edwin Bynner,* Agnes Surriage, *1886*

> *The new Collector of the Port of Boston was regarded as a veritable Prince Charming, and many were the heart-burnings which he caused.*
> — *Edward Robins,* Romances of Early America, *1903*

> *With rank, wealth and high social position as his birthright, with rare personal attractions, and with the endowments which all of these had brought to his aid, Henry Frankland's future bid fair to become unusually dazzling and brilliant.*
> —*Samuel Adams Drake,* New England Legends and Folklore, *1906*

The Frankland family is an old and distinguished line dating back to the eleventh century. Harry's branch stems from the only man to rule England without being crowned: Oliver Cromwell, "The Protector." (Note—Family correspondence almost never uses Charles Henry Frankland's given name. He is known simply as "Harry" or "poor Harry." Nottinghamshire records confusingly refer to both Harry and his father as "Henry Frankland." To avoid confusion, I will refer to him as Harry or Sir Harry.)

Charles Henry Frankland. *Courtesy of the Marblehead Museum and Historical Society.*

Oliver Cromwell's daughter, Frances Cromwell, married Sir John Russell. Their daughter, Elizabeth Russell, Cromwell's granddaughter, married Thomas Frankland.
Henry Frankland, John and Elizabeth's second son, married Mary Cross. Henry and Mary's first son was Charles Henry Frankland.

Harry was born into the landed gentry, a class one step below the aristocracy but—thanks to the beneficence of Henry VIII—one that had the political punch to live like royalty.

When Protestant King Henry confiscated England's Catholic properties in 1530, he rewarded his supporters by giving them large parcels of church land. In so doing, he created a Whig power machine that eventually led to civil war and Cromwell's taking over the government from 1653 to 1658.

The gentry lived in opulent country mansions surrounded by acres of farmland. They were shrewd businessmen: merchants, shipowners and politicians. To augment the income from their enterprises, they collected rent from tenant farmers and sold their crops.

In 1620, Charles II gave William Frankland a baronetcy (making him Sir William). By the English law of primogeniture, William's title and estate, Thirkleby, in the North Riding of Yorkshire passed to each succeeding oldest son: William's son Thomas and then Thomas's son (and Harry's uncle), who was also named Thomas.

Without the promise of an inherited fortune, Harry's father had to find a suitable position. Conveniently, one was created by his uncle John Russell, governor of the East India Company's factory at Fort William in Bengal, India. What could have been more natural in this nepotistic culture than a post for Henry at Fort William?

But the arcane terminology didn't make sense to me. What was the East India Company manufacturing at a "factory" in a far-off place with the name of a military establishment? As I searched for the answer, I gained a new appreciation of the spice trade's tremendous influence on three centuries of European history.

From the beginning of the sixteenth until the middle of the nineteenth centuries, pepper, nutmeg, cinnamon and saltpeter (used in gunpowder manufacture) were the equivalent of oil today. Spices were in heavy demand, with no significant source except India and Asia. Spices not only affected politics and religion, but they also spurred exploration. Spices caused wars, foreign intrigue, smuggling and murder.

Established by Queen Elizabeth in 1600, the British East India Company was a clever hybrid: a government-endorsed monopoly of shrewd London merchants combining the best qualities of nationalization and private enterprise. Driven by their need to reward investors (there were 103 original subscribers, from Sir Steven Soame, the lord mayor of London, to Ralfe Buzbie, grocer),[20] the company's aggressive ship captains armed their vessels and began traveling in convoys to protect their cargo from pirates. For the time being, Parliament looked the other way.

When one of the East India ship captains found a lucrative port, the company bought or rented land from the local government and set up a trading post. On this platform, it established a settlement where native merchants could sell their spices to the company and purchase English manufactured goods—from iron pots to eyeglasses to pistols—at a healthy profit for the company's owners in London.

By the early eighteenth century, these settlements had become "factories" where colonies of "factors," or British trading agents, lived permanently. Working in a company factory was no piece of cake. Threatened from the outside by pirates and the interior by local tribesmen, factories soon became warehouses within the walls of a fort. In time, the British East India Company had its own army and navy.

The system worked. The British East India Company quickly grew into a colossal operation. It had articles of association, stockholders and a board of directors and issued dividends. By 1714, it was capitalized at £3,000,000.[21] By 1720, 15 percent of British imports were from India.[22]

The British East India Company was in the business of trading, not colonization, but a funny thing happened on the way to the market: the factories became colonies, thriving communities with factors and their families, as well as tradesmen, a garrison of soldiers, a hospital and native servants.

Each factory had a governor as the chief civil authority. Supervision of the factories was a direct line from the governor to the "Honorable Court of Directors" in London. The Crown and Parliament were, essentially, out of the loop.

This is the environment into which Charles Henry Frankland was born on May 10, 1716.[23] It was not the greatest place in the world for an infant to arrive. Bengal sits at about the same tropical latitude as Cuba. Fort William was built on a tidal river, surrounded by swamp ground, bordering on a large salt lake. It was hot, dirty and insect- and disease-ridden. On October 13 of the year Harry was born, Robert Hedges, then governor, reported to the directors: "A stinking ditch by Mr. Marche's house must be fill'd up."

I found great confusion in the exact number, sex and birthplaces of Henry Frankland's children, probably because of the distance between England, where their births would have been recorded, and India, where most, if not all, of them were born. Some family histories list five boys and two girls. In 1910, Ralph Frankland Payne-Gallwey, a direct descendant, wrote to the *London Spectator* "condemning" both Elias Nason and Edmund Bynner for the inaccuracies in their books, saying, "Sir Harry had *no* sisters!"

The point could be vigorously argued. Nason identifies as Harry's sisters Anne, Mary and Frances. He says Ann married Thomas Pelham, First Earl of Chichester, but Pelham's wife was Ann, the daughter of Frederic Meinhart Frankland. A pedigree by the British Historical Manuscripts Commission shows Henry Frankland and Mary Cross having only two children, both sons: Sir Charles Henry and Sir Thomas. The same family tree lists a Francis (Fanny) Russell as Harry's cousin, the daughter of John Russell.

There are two references to a sister in Harry's journal. On October 14, 1757, he says: "Write to Mrs. Fanny Russell, my sister" (he may have meant, "Write to Mrs. Fanny Russell, [and] my sister." In the year of his death, 1768, he writes: "My sister's calculation of annual charges in housekeeping."

Some peerage lists have Harry's brother Thomas (not to be confused with his uncle Thomas) born in England. The *Complete Baronage* does not list a birthplace for him but gives his birth date as "about 1718."

The third son of Henry and Mary was born in 1720. His name was William.[24] His existence has been well and carefully documented by Findon Village historian Valerie Martin.

The distance, danger and discomfort involved in sailing to England from Bengal in the eighteenth century would have inhibited Mary Frankland from leaving Calcutta, especially if she were pregnant. An East India Company merchant ship would have to make landfall at one or more of a dozen ports in the Arabian Sea, Indian Ocean and the Atlantic Ocean before reaching England. The need to refresh supplies of food and water, frequent turns of weather and ever-lurking pirates necessitated many unexpected stops along the way.

Sailing from Fort William to England meant at least four and a half to six months of arduous travel. Consider the vicissitudes of a much shorter trip from Boston to London described by Abigail Adams in 1784: "Necessity has no law, but what should I have thought on shore to have laid myself down to sleep in common with a half dozen gentlemen. We have curtains, it is true, and we only partly undress."

And later, in a storm off the Grand Banks: "Some gentleman sat by us with his arm fastened in ours and his feet against a table or chair that was lashed down."[25]

Mary Frankland would have had to cover a total of 10,015 nautical miles—three and a half times the distance traveled by Abigail.

CHAPTER 3

Marblehead, 1732

When Agnes Surriage was six years old, the fishing village of Marblehead was twelve years into a dramatic surge of economic growth: a boom spearheaded not by a merchant king but by a Congregational minister in tandem with a shoemaker.

Parson John Barnard's contributions to the town's commercial independence were almost as significant as his efforts toward its spiritual well-being. He would have stood out among his peers at any time, but in the eighteenth century he was extraordinary.

The man who was once described by Salem's acerbic Reverend William Bentley as "the Bishop of the place [meaning Marblehead]" was born in 1681. After grammar school in Boston, he began his secondary education at Harvard College at the age of fourteen, graduating with honors four years later.

He delivered his first sermon before an informal group of men who met on Sunday evenings to worship and practice preaching. In 1703, Parson Barnard received a master of arts degree from Harvard. By 1709, he was chaplain aboard a British warship. In England, his preaching style was readily accepted, and he delivered many sermons in the Puritan churches there.

Barnard was back in Boston by August 1714, the year he was invited to preach alternately with Edward Holyoke and Amos Cheever at Marblehead's First Church. All three were being considered for the position of assistant to the ailing Samuel Cheever. Not without some controversy—which

The Golden Cod atop
Old North Church.
Photo by the author.

resulted in a schism and establishment of the Second Church under Edward
Holyoke—John Barnard was appointed assistant and presumptive successor
to Cheever in January 1715.

When he arrived as minister of the First Church, Marblehead was a
ramshackle seacoast village. There were an estimated 450 houses. Fishing
supported the town, with more than eighty schooners employing six hundred
men and boys.[26] Dried cod, the town's major product, was sold to merchants
in Salem and Boston, who marked it up and resold it in the West Indies and
European markets for their own profit.

Reverend John was quick to recognize the ripe opportunity that his flock
was missing. The price of prime grade "table cod"—considered a delicacy
in Catholic Europe—was rising with increased demand. "Green cod," or
lower grades of dried fish, were being consumed in great quantities by West
Indies sugar plantations as cheap food for slaves.

The pastor decided to become a self-taught fish merchant. He made a
point of associating with the English ship captains who came to town, "that
I might, by them, be let into the mystery of the fish trade." It did not take
long, as he writes in his autobiography: "When I saw the advantages of it, I
thought it my duty to stir up my people...to send fish to market themselves,
that they might reap the benefit of it, to the enriching [of] themselves,
and serving the town...But alas! I could inspire no man with courage and
resolution enough to engage in it."

Much has been written about Reverend Barnard's role in building the
wealth and stature of Marblehead during the last three quarters of the

eighteenth century, but his little-known partner, Joseph Swett Jr., has been called the man who "put this town on the map."[27]

The only child of Joseph and Hannah (Devereaux) Swett, he was baptized August 25, 1689. Probably by exposure to the many fishermen in town who practiced shoemaking during the winter months, he became a cordwainer (the term used for the trade at the time). Finally, in 1720, at the age of thirty-one, with no experience in the merchant trade, Swett took a leap of faith: he decided to try his luck with John Barnard's plan—a venture that changed the local economy for more than five decades. Again, from the autobiography: "To him I opened myself fully, laid the scheme clearly before him…He first sent a small cargo to Barbados. He soon found he increased his stock, built vessels, and sent the fish to Europe, and prospered in the trade, to the enriching of himself."

Joseph Swett was the first of a social class that became known as the "codfish aristocracy": local merchants selling Marblehead dried cod directly to the southern states, the West Indies and Europe. This group not only replaced the Boston and Salem trade representatives but also attracted a new middle class of merchants, shopkeepers, innkeepers, butchers and tradesmen.

But Agnes Surriage's people—the Marblehead fishermen—remained as poor as ever. And now they were debt ridden.

Here, I received great help from Christine Leigh Heyrman's book, *Commerce and Culture*, which introduced me to the Machiavellian scheme developed by the Marblehead mercantile community to secure their prosperity. "The problem of indebtedness, like that of inequality, was not new to Marblehead…Fishermen defaulting on their debts had created difficulties in town ever since the seventeenth century…But the group that suffered the most were the poorest…who defaulted on their debts and were taken to court by their creditors."[28]

Those merchants to whom the fishermen owed money kept them constantly in hock by bailing them out and then requiring them to work off the loan against their next catch. In addition, the men (and women, for some were merchants also) sold them everything from beef and belt buckles to rum and fishhooks on credit.

It was a literal Catch-22. Those who harvested the ocean had a grim choice: either endure the dangers and uncertainty of pirates, impressment in the British navy, leaky ships and fierce storms for seven months of the year or leave your family destitute while you sit in debtor's prison.

Thus, the very men and boys who gave substance to Marblehead's codfish prosperity became its indentured servants.

CHAPTER 4

Bengal, 1720

Meanwhile, The British East India Company was overwhelming European competitors. One of the major contributions to its success was a unique and unprecedented employee incentive program.

How did the company motivate men like Henry Frankland to live for years in disease-ridden tropical swamplands threatened by local warlords? It simply turned clerks into part-time entrepreneurs by giving them "private trading space" in company ships. The size of each trading space was determined by seniority. Their goods were then sold in London at auction (the company extracting a 15 percent surcharge). It was not unusual for one of these private traders to earn ten times his yearly salary of £120.[29]

Henry Frankland prospered. In 1720, he was able to pay off a £4,000 mortgage on "the Manor...Dissolved Monastery... Mattersey...[and] the rectory of Mattersey [estate]," including all of the miscellaneous cottages, farmlands and buildings on the property.[30] Mattersey, in Robin Hood's Nottinghamshire, became Henry Frankland's absentee owner estate.

On January 30, 1726, he was promoted to governor of the factory.[31]

I was able to obtain a packet of Henry Frankland's letters from the British Library. Surprisingly, they told a fascinating tale of Henry as an unsuccessful eighteenth-century version of a modern corporate whistle-blower.

On January 28, 1726, Henry wrote to the "Honorable Secret Committee" on the affairs of "The Honorable United Company of Merchants of England Trading to the East Indies."[32] The secret committee, I learned, was

Mezzotint engraving of Old Fort William, Bengal. *Courtesy of Wikimedia Commons.*

a kind of eighteenth-century MI-5 composed of Parliamentary spies whose mission was to monitor the company's financial affairs.

His eight-page letter[33] complains of "certain seafaring gentlemen and black merchants [here, probably a term for Indian smugglers]" who were shipping Dutch goods without paying the proper duty. Twenty pages of enclosures accompanied it, describing in detail Henry's plan to prevent this "pernicious practice," which the Secret Committee summarily rejected.

Henry was playing with fire. By jumping into a serious political war between the bureaucrats in Parliament and the directors of the East India Company, he placed himself and his job in jeopardy.

Undaunted, he continued to engage in company politics, this time becoming involved in foreign intrigue. A year later, on January 27, 1727, he wrote again to the Secret Committee, describing his efforts to kidnap a competitor:

> *Our spies, which we have constantly kept on the Ostenders* [the Austrian factory in Bengal], *gave us intelligence that Mr. Hume, with about ten to twelve Europeans, was going up to Cassembazar, upon which we immediately dispatched Lieutenant Wyndham with a party of fifty stout fellows to overtake, and if possible, seize him. Our intelligence happened to be wrong, it not being Mr. Hume, but his brother.*

Later in the same letter, he admits to having "endeavored" to capture Hume several times. This was just plain foolish. Alexander Hume was the governor and commander of the Austrian company called Ostend. He was especially popular with the Muslims in Bengal.

Clearly, Henry was beginning to overstep his bounds. Fort William records contain a directive from London dated February 17, 1727, chastising Frankland for allowing one of the factors (the son of a prominent English coach maker) to pay fines to the local government without "Order of the Council." The language was unusually strong for the reserved style of company communications: "We can never approve of, but do utterly dislike [this behavior] and forbid [it] for the future."[34]

In thirteen months, eleven-year-old Harry's father had managed to infuriate a group of company ship captains, the Dutch, the Austrians, the local Muslims and his own board of directors.

While Henry was busy angering his business associates, he received tragic news about his brother Robert, a government official in Persia. On June 6, 1727, the *Prince George*, an East India Company ship, landed in Jeddah to take ashore the body of a Persian sailor for burial on his home soil. It was a humane gesture designed to quell rumors among the natives that "Musslemen" (Muslim) sailors aboard were being mistreated and murdered by the British crew.

Unfortunately, the pacification attempt was misunderstood, and a mob stormed the house where Robert Frankland was entertaining five other men at dinner. Shouting "Mussleman killed by Twingee," they broke down the doors just as the guests finished eating, killing Robert Frankland and four of his guests.

Henry Frankland died at the age of thirty-eight on August 23, 1728, a short year and eight months after his appointment and five months before the end of his term. He was buried near the church at Fort William.[35] I was not able to find a cause of death in official Fort William records. Three weeks later, his predecessor, John Deane, was named to an unprecedented second term as governor.

I could not help wondering if—given Henry's sudden death and young age—his bother's murder had been an ironic foreshadowing. The governor of the Bengal factory had amassed a robust group of enemies who would benefit from his demise and replacement. Those adversaries were a diverse group, any one of whom had access to the means for what they believed to be Henry's justifiable end.

Twelve-year-old Charles Henry Frankland returned home without a father.

CHAPTER 5

Cast Adrift

Between the ages of twelve and twenty-three, Harry Frankland's life remains a mystery.

Elias Nason, who wrote a credible biography of Sir Harry, claims he was "educated in affluence." But the question remains: where? While three of his Frankland uncles—Frederick, Richard and Thomas—all graduated from King's College,[36] there are no records of Henry or his sons attending Eaton College or matriculating at the University of Oxford, Emanuel or King's Colleges.

Harry's brother Thomas went to sea at the age of fourteen. By the time he was twenty, he had a lieutenant's commission in the Royal Navy.[37] William, another brother, became a wealthy East India trader with a penchant for dangerous, mysterious and quite profitable trips through the Middle East.

In trying to trace Harry's life from 1728 to 1741, I came upon a complete surprise. The following two sentences appeared in a letter from Harry's cousin Fanny to her brother, Lieutenant Colonel Charles Russell, who was with the British army in Prussia: "I dined with Mrs. H. Frankland last Friday. Her son Fred had been to see Mr. Berkley's three sisters." [38]

Suddenly Harry had a third brother. A return letter from Colonel Russell to Fanny on May 31, 1743, further confirmed his existence: "Let Mrs. Frankland know that I have spoken to most of the officers of the regiment on Freddy's behalf, and particularly to Lord Crawford, who, having some obligations to the family, and being very good natured, has promised to countenance him much."[39]

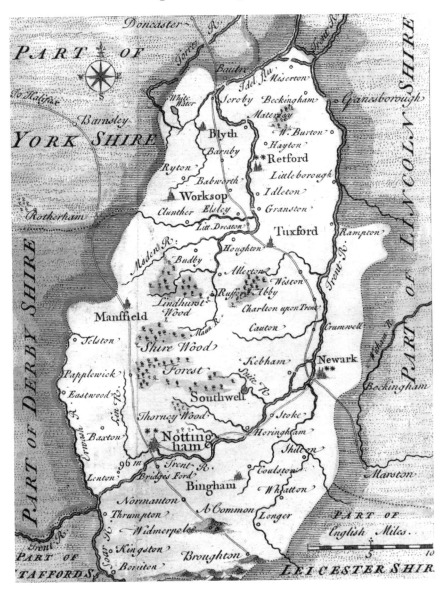

Map of Nottinghamshire drawn in 1742 by Thomas Badeslade (see Mattersey in upper right corner). *Author's collection.*

The operative phrase here is "having some obligations to the family." If there was one thing the landed gentry did well, it was playing politics and using family connections. Lord Crawford's "countenance" got Freddy into Russell's brigade as a "cornet" (bugler).

Thomas Pelham-Holles, First Duke of Newcastle, by William Hoare (circa 1707). *From a print by Philip Mould, London.*

But where is Harry?

After years of searching, I was able to get copies of documents from the Nottinghamshire Archives[40] that began to answer that question. The first, with a date of May 1739, records that "Mary Frankland of Bond Street advances £2,000 to Mr. J. Beckford and Mr. H. Neate for use of Henry [Harry] Frankland of Mattersey."[41]

Another piece of Harry's life showed up in a warrant charging the sheriff of Middlesex County to "take John White and Richard Roe if they be found in his bailiwick, and that he keep them safely so that he may have their bodies before the Lord the King at Westminster on Wednesday next after three weeks of Easter to answer to Henry Frankland Esquire in a plea of trespass."

So who were John White and Richard Row, and what did they have to do with Harry Frankland?

A man named John White represented the Nottinghamshire county of Retford in the House of Commons for the years 1735, 1741 and 1754. He would definitely have been one of the Franklands' Mattersey neighbors, a friend of Uncle Thomas and Uncle Frederick Meinhart Frankland.

Richard Roe offers more interesting possibilities. Like "John Doe," this name is traditionally assigned to a party in a legal action when the person's real identity is not known or cannot be revealed because of age, privacy or delicacy. It is reasonable to assume that Richard Roe was not the actual name of the second defendant.

In eighteenth-century court records, "trespass" is often used in the biblical sense. It can refer to a broad range of crimes, from encroaching on someone's property to blackmail or slander. Whatever the reason for the court case, or its outcome, Harry turns up in Boston three and a half months later.

Chapter 6

A Snow Named *Hawke*

At the Phillips Library in Salem, I discovered the original copy of an agreement between "John Waters and Josepth Gliden, of Boston, shipwrights" and "Henry Frankland and Robert Lightfoot, also of Boston" to build a snow-rigged merchant ship.[42] It was to be "fifty-four feet in length by the keel…twenty-one and a half feet in breadth at the beam…eleven-feet deep in the hold." There can be no doubt that this was a ship for carrying goods to Europe and the West Indies.

The agreement has a date of September 28, 1739, and contains a stipulation to "safely launch her in the water on or before the "first day of May next [1740]." Frankland and Lightfoot would pay £100 at the signing of the agreement, the total price of the snow to be calculated on its tonnage at completion and "paid two-thirds money and one-third goods."

On October 10, 1739, the *Boston Gazette* ran the following: "To be sold by Messrs Frankland & Lightfoot at their warehouse in Doctor Cook's building letter D. All sort of cordage from Ratline of one inch to cables of eight inches. Also Spanish and Yorkshire cloths, and most other European and East India Goods, all lately imported."

A third document, dated November 1739, records that Henry Frankland, Esq.—who is described as "late of Mattersey in the county of Nottingham, now of Boston in the County of Suffolk in the Province of the Massachusetts Bay"—made a letter of attorney empowering his uncle Frederick and mother to collect and hold all rents on his properties, execute leases and receive "all sums of money" due him. A power of attorney usually indicates that the

Snow in a storm. *Drawing by Ashley Bowen, courtesy of the Marblehead Museum and Historical Society.*

principal is unable to carry out legal or financial transactions through death, sickness or mental instability. At this point in his life, Harry seemed alive and well, so the obvious conclusion is that he planned to be in America for an extended visit and agreed to his mother and uncle Freddie handling his affairs in England.

But eight months later, Harry sounds bored and depressed in a letter to Thomas Howles, Duke of Newcastle, the most powerful man in Nottingham, who had direct links to Prime Minister Robert Walpole:

> *Boston New England*
> *May 19: 1740*
> *My Lord Duke*
>
> *...I was very Sorry Your Grace would not grant me a lease of Martin in Nottinghamshire & cannot conceive the reason why my Lord Galloway opposed me so much in that request since all the Gentlemen of that part of the Country were so very desirous of my Sett. [settling] there in order to strengthen the Whig interest. I have desired Mr. White to acquaint Your Grace with this affair, & hope Your Grace will grant me a lease of it, at the Expiration of Bank's.*
>
> *By that time, I believe I shall return to Old England, for tho this is the finest Country & Climate I ever saw, Yet I begin to grow Sick of the people.*

I hope my Lord you will pardon this freedom, & if your Grace will honor me, with any Commands here, they shall be punctually obey'd, being with great respect

Your Graces <u>Most</u> Obed' & hum serv
Henry Frankland

There is no record of a reply from the duke.

I found a surprising new addition to the merchant fleet of Frankland and Lightfoot while reading the personal log of Peter Vezian, quartermaster on a British privateer named *Revenge*. Vezian tells of returning to Providence, Rhode Island, with a British sloop recaptured from the Spanish. He recounts the events of Thursday night, August 13, 1741, when a lightning bolt "struck our mast & shivered it very much, besides tearing a large piece off the hounds. As it fell, it tore up the bitts, broke in the hatch way, and burst through both our sides."

From Vezian's journal: "Friday, August 14th 1741—This morning came on board Cap't Frankland to see the misfortune we had suffered the night before, & offered to assist us in all he could. He sent his carpenter, who viewed the mast & said he thought he could make it do again."

Captain Frankland was Harry's younger brother Thomas, who had recently taken command of the HMS *Rose*, also stationed in Providence. But his eagerness to assist the *Revenge*'s captain seems to have been prompted by a hidden agenda:

Thursday, 27th—Got all our sails & powder from on shore, and took an inventory of the prize's rigging and furniture, as she was to be sold Saturday next. Capt Frankland came on board to view her, intending to buy her, I believe.
Saturday, 29th—Today the sloop & furniture was sold, & bought by Cap't Frankland.

Three days later, the privateer's captain settled his affairs in Providence and "took bills of Exchange of Captain Frankland on his brother, Messrs. Frankland & Lightfoot, merchants in Boston." So late in the summer of 1741, Frankland and his business partner were paying for a sloop procured by his brother.

One rainy afternoon, I was in the Marblehead Museum Historical Society's library browsing through the 250-year-old journal of Ashley

Bowen, a colorful Marblehead mariner.[43] It was all I could do to resist letting out a triumphal whoop when I read this entry: "I was bound the 15 of April [1742] to Captain Peter Hall of Boston to serve him seven years. He then commanded a fine snow called the *Hawke*, after Captain Edward Hawke, then Commander of His Majesty's Ship *Portland*, then at Boston and owned by Sir Harry Frankland, a native of England." This was undoubtedly the snow built for Harry and Robert Lightfoot launched in May 1740.

From September 1739 to April 1742, Harry had been busy acquiring a partner, buying ships and trading in the West Indies. According to S.D. Smith, author of *Slavery, Family, and Gentry Capitalism in the British Atlantic*,[44] he was following a long-standing family tradition. In his book, Smith connects the Franklands directly to long-term involvement in the mercantile life of Barbados: "The Franklands have been largely absent from accounts of colonial history, but they were remarkably active in eighteenth century commerce. By 1786, the family had probably been connected with Barbados for more than a century."

Smith links Harry's brother Thomas to slave trader Gedney Clark, who worked the Triangle Trade route between the continents of North America, Africa and the West Indies. Between the years of 1738 and 1745 they were dealing in fish and whale oil in exchange for sugar and rum. Clark is listed in the ledgers of not only Timothy Orne, in Salem, but also Marblehead's Joseph Swett and Robert Hooper, all of whom "were involved in a network of merchant correspondents based in Europe, North America, and the Caribbean."[45]

The *Hawke*'s trip of 1742 took it to Philadelphia, and then, according to Bowen, it "lay at St. Eustace [St. Eustatius] with molasses." From the West Indies, the *Hawke* returned to Cape Ann (Gloucester) in March 1743 to offload cargo. Bad news greeted Captain Hall and his crew on their arrival. Bowen writes: "When we arrived at Cape Ann and run our cargo of fruit and wines, and there was a great noise about it as about this time a vessel was informed against and Sir Harry was obliged to take notice of her and seized her and the concerned swore vengeance against our snow."

But Harry's troubles had just begun. From Cape Ann, the *Hawke* went south to Marblehead, where the thirteen-year-old cabin boy noted a disturbance over Frankland's status: "Our owner being a collector and his vessel at the same time a-running goods made some difficulty."

Thank you, Ashley Bowen. If Frankland and Lightfoot were buying molasses at a Dutch Island, they had to be selling dried cod in the process.

Considering Harry's inside knowledge of the market, he would have dealt with his brother's friends Swett and Hooper in Marblehead.

That Harry was trading in fish, molasses, rum and naval stores while holding the position of king's collector was new and somewhat surprising information. The legends have always positioned him as a wealthy nobleman, certainly not the profile of a dealer in goods. Instead of the "royal lover" that Oliver Wendell Holmes described, ready to "woo without the ring and book," I had discovered the son of a gentry capitalist family who was double dipping as a government official and a triangle-trading merchant.

CHAPTER 7

The Fort

While supervising the erection of Fort Sewall, he met Agnes Surriage.
—historical marker at the corner of Orne Street and Fountain Inn Lane

From reading his journal, I found it hard to imagine that Harry Frankland's interests and experience (horticulture, cooking, medicine for gout, philosophical aphorisms) would qualify him for supervising the construction of a fort. Why would William Shirley, who knew his background well, send Harry to oversee the work in Marblehead?

Or did he? It's time to take a second look at this reconstruction of the fort.

First, its location: Marblehead Harbor is bounded on the southeast by Marblehead neck. A narrow strip of land—today called the causeway—connecting this peninsula to the mainland forms the head. The mouth of the harbor opens to the east, between the neck and the town. Early fishing vessels moored in Little Harbor, a small cove to the north of the "Great Harbor," as it was called in the eighteenth century.

The most strategic point for the Great Harbor's defense is a headland that rises sharply out of the ocean between the two bodies of water. Known as "Gale's Head," it was donated to the town in the seventeenth century by Ambrose Gale,[46] a civic-minded landowner. About 1666, some cannons were placed there, but by the mid-eighteenth century, after seventy-five years of neglect, the fort was in a state of disrepair.

To French and Dutch pirates, the free flow of money and goods through a growing and unprotected fishing port close to Boston was as attractive

Ammunition magazine, Fort Sewall. *Photo by the author.*

Top left: Marblehead neck. *Top right*: Causeway. *Center*: Mouth of Marblehead Harbor. *Bottom*: Fort Sewall, Little Harbor and Gerry (Priest's) Island. *Photo by Rick Ashley.*

Past meets present: Glover's Marblehead regiment encampment at Fort Sewall against a harbor full of pleasure craft. *Photo by the author.*

as an uncovered candle flame to a swarm of moths. So it is not surprising that, by 1727—a scant year after Agnes was born—Marblehead's town fathers had become extremely concerned. Twenty-three prominent shipowners, merchants and landsmen (including Nathaniel Bartlett, owner of the Fountain Inn) petitioned the Great and General Court for funds in a document that was a masterpiece of colonial hard sell.

It declared Marblehead to be "the special part of one of the greatest branches of our trade...so nearly situated to the great merchandise for Boston" and then added a grim note of caution: "no owner will chance that his vessel shall ride in so insecure a place." Winding up with a strong urge to action, these hucksters in three-cornered hats and knee britches concluded, "All of which seems to require a suitable guard and defense for the harbor, when there is often ten to twenty sail of ship of trade besides more than a hundred sail of fishing vessels."

It took fifteen years for the court to do anything about the defense of Marblehead. On April 10, 1742, it appropriated £550 for the construction of a "good and sufficient Breast Work and a Platform built, and twelve Guns twelve Pounders or others equivalent mounted."

One would assume the news from Boston would be cause for celebration in Marblehead. Instead, the voting public became paranoid about such a large sum of money. Town meeting elected a committee of five men to receive the funds directly from Governor Shirley, with instructions to turn it over to three other citizens who had been selected as treasurers.

The money was placed in an ironbound chest with two locks. But to ensure its security, town meeting again voted that the chest was not to be opened unless all three treasurers were present. Two of the treasurers immediately resigned, leaving Joseph Swett as lone custodian of the funds. Thomas Gerry and Nathan Bowen (Ashley's father) were chosen as replacements, and work on the fort began, presumably in the fall of 1742.

There is no mention of Harry Frankland in connection with Marblehead's fort in the journals of the Massachusetts House of Representatives for 1741 to 1743. However, I found a possible reason for the popular belief that he had been involved in its construction. On September 13, 1742, the *Boston Post Boy* carried an article reporting, "His Excellency, our Captain General [Governor Shirley] set out from hence to view and appoint the places for erecting the new batteries in the towns of Charlestown, Salem, and Marblehead."

The article describes a ceremonial tour worthy of a modern political campaign. In each town, "Four companies of foot under Arms, who discharged three vollies," greeted Shirley, followed by salutes from the fort's cannons accompanied by all the church bells in town. The king's collector would have been a logical member of the governor's party. If so, it could account for Harry's legendary reputation as construction supervisor.

On March 2, 1743, Shirley wrote the House requesting payment for: "Mr. Bastide, His Majesty's Engineer...[who] has viewed the ground upon which I proposed to erect the several Batteries at Marblehead, Cape Ann, and Falmouth in Casco Bay, and projected the same, and drawn out plans for the works, and given the necessary directions for carrying them on." A reasonable conclusion is that Mr. Bastide, the engineer—not Harry Frankland, the gentrified merchant—supervised the construction of Fort Sewall in 1742.

I was still left with a historical marker claiming that "Sir Harry Frankland" (an inaccuracy, since he didn't receive the title until 1747) supervised the "erection of Fort Sewall." The sign looked official and sounded authoritative. What was the Massachusetts Tercentenary Commission? Where did it get its facts?

As the name implies, the commission was an organization made up of state and town governments created in 1930 to celebrate the 300th anniversary of the Massachusetts Bay Charter. However, its mission seems to have been more promotional than educational. Author James Bodnar, who wrote extensively about celebration and patriotism in the twentieth century, indicates that it grew out of a desire to boost morale during the Depression by reviving civic pride in the history of the state. The Tercentenary Commission planned and executed over two thousand separate events involving eleven million people.[47] According to commission chairman Herbert Parker, the function of the signs was to "tell of the heroism, of the romance, and of the tragedies...of the ancestors of our commonwealth."[48]

My best guess is that whoever wrote the inscription on the well marker simply condensed the prevailing version of the legend.

If the collector was in Marblehead, he was there for other business than protection of the harbor.

CHAPTER 8

"Th' Fuhtn"

E arly Marblehead's most famous hostelry grew from deceptively humble
roots.[49] Construction began when Nathaniel Bartlett dug a big hole
in his father's front lawn close to the "Fountain Well," so named because
it was originally an underground spring that bubbled out of the ground
like a fountain. The date can be pinpointed by a January 7, 1720/1 deed
of William Bartlett, yeoman and fisherman, and his wife, Sarah, to their
son, Nathaniel, for "a small piece of land where his cellar is now in our
orchard."[50] Three years later, Bartlett's uncle, Nathaniel Walton, died and
left him a piece of land where "he hath set up a new house," indicating that
the inn had been built and was accepting guests by 1723.

Nathaniel Bartlett's establishment became known as the Fountain Tavern.
Existing buildings of the same era suggest that it would have been a two-story
structure with about eight rooms. "Th' Fuhtn," as early Headers might have
chopped and pronounced its name, sat high on a plateau forty feet above the
southern shore of Little Harbor directly across from the fort. This plateau
is actually the first of three huge steps. The second is formed by a towering
rock ledge that rises steeply to another slab of land, today known as Fountain
Park. From there, the terrain ascends over immense granite outcroppings to
the peak of the Burial Hill, where Marblehead's first meetinghouse stood.

The location commands a stunning panorama of nearly 180 degrees,
stretching from the southeasterly end of Fort Sewall northeast to Baker's
Island off Salem Harbor. In 1909, historian Nathan Sanborn rhapsodized,
"It is as grand and beautiful an outlook as ever came within the range of

The Fountain Inn.

mortal vision."[51] However, Bartlett, like most of our ancestors, attached little value to a water view. From the location of sun-dried bricks unearthed near the well, probably from the tavern's colonial fireplace, we can conclude that Nathaniel built his inn for access: its back to the harbor and front door dead center in the lane that extended to the main road.

For many years, the Fountain Tavern was the only place in town where a weary traveler could find a place to stay. In addition to visitors from foreign ports, the gentry of New England towns near and far sought a drop of rum and a night's sleep under its roof. In addition, the tavern was a popular gathering place where wealthy merchants and local fishermen alike emptied their mugs over talk of storms at sea, the price of smoked cod and town gossip. According to their records, the "Commoners," who were predecessors of the selectmen, held their meetings at the tavern.

Romantic tales of pirates reveling at the Fountain Tavern abound, but the only factual evidence[52] of a pirate actually being in Marblehead predates Nathaniel Bartlett. A proclamation issued in 1703 by Lieutenant Governor Povey commands "all officers, civil and military to apprehend… John Quelch, the captain of the privateer ship *Charles* [which had recently landed in Marblehead] for felony and piracy." Samuel Roads states that "there were those living who remembered" Quelch's arrest on the streets of Marblehead.[53]

PART II
Lust

CHAPTER 9

Smuggling, Bribery and Puberty

We're forbidden to trade in France or in Spain,
We cannot have commerce with Fin, Swede, or Dane,
Taxing the industrious, England gains control…
Give me the punch ladle; I'll fathom the bowl.
—colonial parody of an eighteenth-century English tavern song

The townies who sang these bitter words as they quaffed their rum at the Fountain Tavern had a legitimate gripe: they were stuck in the middle of an ongoing trade war between Britain, France, the Dutch Republic and Spain.

In 1651, Parliament passed the Navigation Acts. These restrictive laws, designed to protect British trade routes, prohibited the transport of goods to England from Asia, Africa or America except in English vessels. It also required that goods of any European country imported into England must be brought in British vessels or in vessels of the country producing them.

As strict as the acts were, they couldn't prevent the French from being better at growing sugar cane and selling it at low prices. In the first quarter of the eighteenth century, a brisk trade had developed between the colonies and the French Islands, to the exclusion of the British West Indies.

Parliament—spurred by British plantation owners—produced another suppressive measure: the Molasses Act of 1733. It imposed outrageous duties of six pence per gallon on molasses, nine pence per gallon on rum and five shillings for every one hundred weight of sugar imported to North

Drying Fish, Little Harbor. *Courtesy of Sun Publishing Co.*

America from non-British colonies. The intent was to restore trade taken from the British West Indies by the French. The immediate result, however, was a burgeoning illicit trade.

The Molasses Act levy had to be paid before ships were allowed to land. This put tremendous power in the hands of Harry Frankland and his fellow collectors. As the king's representatives in the colonies, they were responsible for inspecting the cargo of each arriving vessel and ensuring that its tariff was paid. The result of placing government officials in a perfect position to receive bribes from rich businessmen was inevitable: an outbreak of what has been arguably called "the second oldest profession."

Marblehead's deep mile-long harbor, the temperament of its feisty hard-drinking residents and the sudden influx of a nouveau riche quickly positioned it as the smuggling port for Boston and an integral part of a highly organized underground economy.

Marblehead sloops sold premium dried fish in Europe and imported the large amounts of salt required to cure cod from Portugal. The French and Dutch islands of Guadeloupe, Martinique and Haiti were regular sources of molasses, sugar and rum. Ship captains deftly changed the records on their return. Boston merchants had their contraband offloaded in Marblehead before officially returning home. And the colonists were not alone. When it came to smuggling, the Brits were equally talented: 80 percent of the tea they drank had been slipped into the country without duty payment.[54]

The correspondence of Robert Hooper and Joseph Swett[55] indicates that they were involved in a network of European, North American and Caribbean merchants. But smuggling was not just an avocation of the wealthy. To get a barrel of Barbados molasses or a bag of "La Grenade" sugar from the West Indies to a cellar hiding place in Marblehead took not only captains and crews but also clerks in the customhouse and dockworkers. Just about everyone in town was involved, one way or another.

Marblehead had become the gathering place for those who had every reason to flout Britain's restrictive mercantile laws. The king's collectors eagerly, if covertly, accepted bribes. Historian George Bancroft observed: "The officers of the custom used to permit evasions of the law as the only means of acquiring wealth."[56]

For years, Marbleheaders have theorized about secret places tucked away behind trapdoors and loose floorboards to hide goods illegally transported from Europe, the West Indies and Africa. Cellars of historic houses have been scoured for hidden passageways that might have led to tunnels that snaked and twisted their way to dark places under wharves and in tiny coves. Real evidence is hard to find, but considering the existing strictures on trade, these suppositions have a sound of credibility.

Christine Leigh Heyrman observes in *Commerce and Culture* that "half of the richest quintile and over half of the top ten percent of the town's rate payers in 1748 attended the First Church." A shrewd John Barnard, who had been offered partnerships by "considerable merchants" before leaving England,[57] would have embraced Marblehead's prosperity. Throughout his career, he demonstrated a superb sense of pragmatism in both ecumenical and secular matters.

The year is 1741.

Immersed in this milieu of smuggling and bribery is a pubescent Agnes Surriage.

CHAPTER 10

Fair Game

It seems to have been taken for granted that maidservants were fair game for men's advances: the men were not the worse thought of—so long as they made arrangements for any bastards that resulted.
—John Atkins, *Sex in Literature*

Eighteenth-century English gentlemen of the upper classes were supercharged with blatant eroticism. Roy Porter, lecturer in social history of medicine at the Wellcome Institute for the History of Medicine in London, sums up the ambience of Harry's world: "Perhaps the most marked feature about Georgian Sexuality was its public nature, its openness and visibility." Porter quotes Samuel Johnson's biographer, James Boswell: "At the bottom of Haymarket I picked up a strong, jolly young damsel, and taking her under the arm I conducted her to Westminster Bridge, and then in amour complete did I engage her upon this noble edifice. The whim of doing it there with the Thames rolling below us amused me very much."[58]

The Age of Enlightenment had begun to question religious dogma. Cause and effect were replacing the hand of God in the order of nature. Newton predicted the movement of planets governed by mathematical laws. John Locke used Newtonian physics to describe the brain and nerves as a mechanical system driven by the five senses. It was only a short step to the definition of sex as a natural sensation, an "essential part of nature…an important component of happiness."

The result was that Englishmen of Harry's generation were constantly exposed to sexual stimulation: in both high-class and popular pornography, the low décolletage worn by women, the predominance of prostitutes on the streets of London and the casual nature of public sex.[59]

Paradoxically, the mid-eighteenth century was inundated by a veritable tsunami of romantic sentimentality. Harry would probably have decried pure animal sex. Although driven by the hormones of our Neanderthal ancestors, his behavior would have been modified by the artful passion of a Casanova. In order to be enjoyable, sex had to be "refined, decent, polite."

A contemporary Dutch immigrant, Bernard Mandeville, observed the special kind of jeopardy faced by women in menial positions: "Lower class women were particularly vulnerable to being seduced and abandoned by a 'Powerful Deceiver.' Thus made pregnant, a woman's sorrows were 'unspeakable.' It was under those circumstances that she might make away with the child."[60]

The Chocolate Girl (oil on canvas), Liotard, Jean-Etienne (1702–89) (after) / Galleria Palatina, Palazzo Pitti, Florence, Italy. *The Bridgeman Art Library International.*

In stark contrast, Agnes would have been under the influence of a totally different sexual paradigm. As her young body began stirring to the changes of puberty, a cultural phenomenon called the Great Awakening swept into Marblehead like a contagious disease. Enlightenment thinking did not sit well with the Calvinism of more conservative New England. The faithful believed that as descendants of original sin, we dangle over the fires of hell on a thin thread held by the hand of God. He alone controlled our fate: He alone determined who would enter the Kingdom of Heaven and who would fall below. Those who strenuously followed the will of God were more likely to be elevated to Heaven. Others descended into eternal flames.

However, by 1740, the younger generation was shedding the piety of its Puritan predecessors. The alarm caused by their coed parties, wagon rides under quilts at night and a shocking increase in children conceived out of wedlock created a ready audience.

Preachers like Jonathan Edwards—a Yale graduate called by the people of Northampton, Massachusetts, in 1726—were adapting their more or less dry, conservative preaching to include a more revivalist emotionalism. It has been described as "sensualized spirituality."[61] Edwards told his parishioners in tones that were measured but emotionally charged: "Family government did too much fail in the town…where most frolicking is carried on, there are the most frequent breaking out of gross sins; fornication in particular."[62]

A surprising thing happened. When Edwards told congregations that it was in God's power to save whomever He pleases, they interpreted it as: "If you try, God will aid your salvation."[63] Whether they were driven by a suggestive reaction to his hypnotic monotone or their own anxiety, listeners began to experience dramatic conversions: barking, speaking in tongues and running in circles.

The Great Awakening was spotty, breaking out in different settlements at different times. It came to Marblehead in 1737 when Agnes was eleven years old. By that time, the liberal-minded Edward Holyoke had left Second Church to become the ninth president of Harvard University.

There was no reason to expect that his replacement, Simon Bradstreet, would bring change with him. His grandmother, Anne Bradstreet, is remembered as America's first female poet. His father, a Harvard graduate, was a noted liberal minister in Charlestown. Like Holyoke, Simon had graduated from Harvard, but that's where all similarity ended. To the rough, tough fishing town of Marblehead, where revivalist evangelism was virtually unknown, Simon Bradstreet brought a strict Calvinist theology.

One would have expected a riot.

Instead, Bradstreet's congregation grew. From the time of Holyoke's departure in 1738 to 1742, membership of the Second Church almost doubled. Assertive, lower-class women led the charge. Fishermen's wives presided over afternoon prayer meetings. Affluent merchants and tradesmen became involved. Even pragmatic John Barnard adapted his First Church sermons to project a more evangelical tone.[64]

Not everyone at Second Church welcomed the Great Awakening. Nathan Bowen left, joining St. Michaels, saying that he was outraged that "women and common negroes take upon them to extort their Betters in the pulpit."[65] Defections like Bowen's were frequent enough to be noticed by the Episcopal laity. I found this quote from a prominent member of King's Chapel in J.A. Doyle's *The Colonies under the House of Hanover*: "There are clerical witnesses, possibly prejudiced. But we find a layman, Sir Henry Frankland, also stating that the effect of Whitfield's teaching has been to dispose 'the sober sort of Dissenters' to join the church."[66] Harry was referring to George Whitefield (pronounced Whitfield), acknowledged as the most famous itinerant minister of the Great Awakening.

At 11:00 a.m. on Monday, September 29, 1740—in the autumn of Agnes's fourteenth year—Whitefield preached in Marblehead. If Jonathan Edwards was the first violin of the movement, George Whitefield was its tuba section. He was a large, rotund man with a booming stentorian voice. In spite of a squint, which rendered his eyes barely visible, he could hold an audience of thousands spellbound.

No less than that old scientist, nonsectarian, deist Benjamin Franklin was one of his admirers (but certainly not one of his followers). In his autobiography, Franklin described Whitefield's clarion call: "He had a loud and clear voice, and articulated his words and sentences so perfectly, that he might be heard and understood at a great distance…I computed that he might be well heard by more than thirty thousand."[67]

Whitefield's journal reported that in Marblehead he "spoke to thousands in a broad place in the middle of town." This was perhaps Training Field Hill, the present-day site of Abbot Hall, or Market Square, in front of the town hall (Old Town House).

His estimate of thousands may be questionable, but if young Agnes had been among them, she would have been exposed to a thundering mantra of abstinence: "Lust had conceived in Eve's heart; shortly it will bring forth sin. Sin, being conceived, brings forth death. Come, haste ye away and walk with God, and make no longer provision for the flesh, to fulfill the lust thereof."

CUT TO: Exterior: the Fountain Inn. Agnes Surriage is on her hands and knees scrubbing the steps.

ENTER: Harry Frankland, English gentleman of the landed gentry, who has called himself "dissolute"[68]—an unusual word for self-description in any century. Its definition gives us a clear indication of his self-image: "dissipated and immoral, profligate, licentious…lacking in restraint."

CLOSE UP: Agnes, daughter of the God-fearing but fiercely self-willed codfish widows. Without doubt, she would have looked at him in awe. Here was the personification of royalty standing before her—talking to her! Inbred class consciousness would have given her an immediate and overwhelming sense of complete inferiority. She was a poor servant girl chopping wood and emptying slop buckets.

Did Charles Henry Frankland feel compassion for a spirited, threadbare waif? Or did he feel desire for a robust young wench with whom he fancied "playing the rogue"?

Of one thing we can be certain: the young maid had no idea that she was fair game.

CHAPTER 11

Accidental Pawn?

Marblehead residents of the twenty-first century, who see their town as a sequestered suburb of Boston, have a hard time visualizing the immensity of its commercial traffic in the 1740s. Not only was Marblehead the third-largest port of entry after Boston and Salem, but it also exported more cured fish than all of New England combined.

Any change in the enforcement of import/export regulations—a new collector in Boston, for example—would have created quite a stir. There would be hushed conferences at the customhouse down by the town landing, in parlors along King Street and at the Fountain Inn.

Men like Robert Hooper and Joseph Swett—Marblehead's leading dried fish exporters—had a reason to be concerned about the new arrival's approach to enforcing trade restrictions. Would he wink and look the other way (with his hand extended palm up) as his predecessors had?

Familiarity may have alleviated their fears somewhat. Harry Frankland, of Frankland and Lightfoot, was no stranger in town. As owner of the *Hawke* (and possibly other merchant vessels), he probably had been buying cod here since early 1740. In some respects, he was a codfish aristocrat himself. And, as Ashley Bowen observed, there were those in town who were none too happy that he was the collecting tariff while running codfish in competition with the local merchants.

There is no primary record of Harry Frankland's first meeting with Agnes Surriage. Not only the date but also the details of their encounter have come to us second and third hand, " according to family tradition."[69] We will never know the truth. The only fact concerning this event is that Harry would have had reason to stay at the Fountain Inn anytime after the establishment of Frankland and Lightfoot in October 1739.

His attraction to Agnes would not have escaped notice. Innkeeper Nathaniel Bartlett had ample opportunity to observe the British gentleman's reaction to his serving girl. Harry's important position gave Bartlett a ready motivation to spread this valuable scuttlebutt among his more elite friends and customers. Who could resist watching the amazed and amused reaction of the codfish aristocracy when they learned that the new collector from Boston couldn't take his eyes off Ed Surriage's daughter?

More than one of the shrewd merchants in town would be mulling over ways to use Harry's indiscretion for personal advantage. The dignity and stature of the king's agent could only be diminished by information (factual or embellished) about his dalliance with a tavern girl.

But there's a strong possibility that at least one other person in town greeted the gossip from the Fountain Inn with anticipation. Mary Pierce Surriage believed that her great-grandfather, John Brown, had owned extensive property in Pemaquid. A proud woman who thought she had married beneath herself could have greeted the gossip about her daughter and the gentleman of Nottingham with a nascent feeling of redemption.

CHAPTER 12

Henry Cromwell

No one has ever seriously tackled the subject of Henry Cromwell, Sir Charles Henry Frankland's natural son, yet he plays a pivotal role in Agnes Surriage's life. Frankland's biographer, Elias Nason, suddenly materializes Henry as a boy of "about twelve" who mysteriously joins Harry and Agnes at their Hopkinton estate in 1752. He offers no explanation of the boy's conception, birth or infancy.[70]

Edwin Bynner's 1898 romantic fiction novel, *Agnes Surriage*,[71] completely ignores this part of the story, probably the result of Victorian propriety. *Lady Good-for-Nothing*, Arthur Quiller Couch's 1910 fictional version of the legend, contains a child born out of wedlock named Dickie Vyell who appears to be six or seven years of age when his father, Captain Oliver Vyell (Harry Frankland), meets Ruth Josselin (Agnes Surriage).[72]

That Charles Henry Frankland fathered him is a matter of record.[73] The mystery surrounding Henry Cromwell is the identity of his birth mother.

I did find one historian who questioned Harry's paternity. A paper on John Rowe, a Boston merchant, read before the Massachusetts Historical Society by Edward L. Pierce on March 14, 1895, contains an interesting idea: "Henry Cromwell's identity is involved in obscurity. Sir Charles Henry Frankland is usually named as his putative father, but the history, which comes nearest the time, makes him the natural son of Sir Thomas Frankland, Sir Charles' Uncle and immediate predecessor to the title. No writer makes any suggestion as to his maternity."

His "history which comes nearest the time" is *Memoirs of the Protectoral House of Cromwell*, written in 1784 by Mark Noble, who is not as positive about Henry's paternity: "Sir Thomas had a natural son, to whom he gave the name Henry Cromwell, as I am credibly informed."

Since Henry Cromwell was still living at the time of Noble's writing, he would be the most likely "credible" informant. However, I find this highly unlikely, since Noble later identifies Sir Harry's wife as the "former Agnes Brown" (a mistake Henry would have corrected immediately). In truth, Sir Thomas held little regard for Harry, resenting the fact that since he had no son, the law of primogeniture made his nephew successor to the baronetcy. It is inconceivable that he would have surrendered his flesh and blood to the collector.

In *Dame Agnes Frankland and Some Chichester Contemporaries*, a monograph written for the Chichester City Council in 1964, Stella Palmer writes: "Henry Cromwell…was an illegitimate son of Sir Harry's, born in England in 1741. His mother is unknown." Palmer does not cite a source for her conclusion that Henry was born in England.

However, a direct descendant of Harry Frankland's seems quite certain of Henry Cromwell's mother. Discussing Agnes Surriage in a 1910 letter,[74] Ralph Frankland Payne-Gallwey says: "Her [Agnes Surriage's] son, before marriage, became Admiral Henry Cromwell." He references a handwritten family pedigree in the Yorkshire Archaeological Society[75] that refers to Henry Cromwell as the "natural son of…Sir Harry and Agnes Surriage."

Without personal letters, court records or contemporary newspaper references, it is difficult, if not impossible, to find the mother of a child born out of wedlock more than two hundred years ago. Doctors and midwives were not required to report their deliveries. Baptism was out of the question, so official data are virtually nonexistent.

I decided that the only way to make an educated guess about Henry Cromwell's mother would be to find out when he was born, roughly calculate the time of his conception and try to pinpoint Harry's location at that time. My search for an answer took me back two thousand years to AD 43, when Julius Caesar governed England. The Romans brought the Julian calendar and England hung on to it, even when Pope Gregory introduced his Gregorian calendar in the sixteenth century. In 1582, when all Catholic and most Protestant countries in Europe changed their way of marking the year, England and its colonies would have nothing to do with Rome telling them what day it was. In 1752, 170 years later, an act of Parliament finally brought the Gregorian calendar to England.

The importance of this chronological detail is that, like many people born before 1752, Henry Cromwell had two birthdays. Widespread confusion has resulted from two adjustments that have to be made in order to accommodate the differences in Julian and Gregorian dates:

1. The Gregorian calendar added eleven days to the Julian calendar.

2. England and its colonies insisted on starting the New Year on March 25 instead of January 1.

George Washington is a famous example. He was born on February 11, 1731, by the Julian calendar. But because 1731 ended on December 31 in the Gregorian calendar—and after 1752 eleven days were added to the date—his birthday is now February 22, 1732.

We can see how this confounded Harry Frankland from two cryptic entries in his personal journal.[76] (Although Harry spells Sally's surname "McClister," I have followed Nason and others who use the more accepted "McClester." He also refers to his son as Harry, although everyone else called him Henry.) The first appears on August 25, 1756 (below):

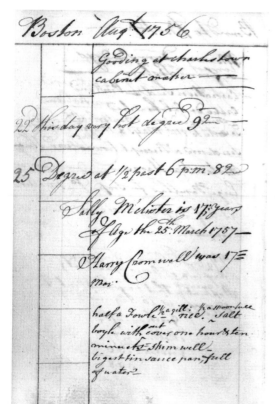

"Sally M'Clister is 17 years of age the 25th March, 1757. Harry Cromwell was 17= [three horizontal quill strokes] Mar."
Courtesy of Massachusetts Historical Society.

Sally was Agnes's niece, the daughter of Mary Surrage McClester, both of whom lived with Harry and Agnes at Hopkinton. This entry in the journal leaves no doubt that she will be seventeen years old in 1757. The date, March 25, is ambiguous. It could have been a reference to either New Year's Day in the English calendar or Sally's actual birthday. The note about Henry Cromwell is less clear. Did the past tense "was" mean that he was seventeen in March 1756, making Henry a year older than Sally?

The mystery deepens. Two months later, on October 23, 1756, Harry writes: "Harry Cromwell went to Piscataqua with Capt. M'Daniel in order to go aboard his majesty's ship Success, Capt. Rouse, at Casco Bay. Harry Cromwell is 16 years of age next February."

When Harry made those entries four years after the change of calendars, I believe he was struggling to conform ages to dates. Did he calculate that Henry Cromwell was seventeen in the August entry and then correct himself in October?

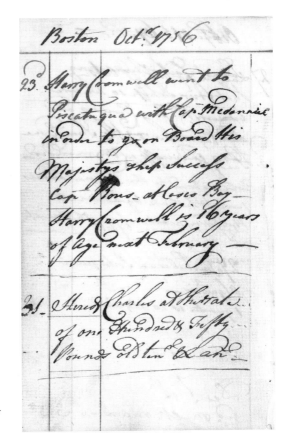

"Henry Cromewell is 16 years of age next February." *Courtesy of Massachusetts Historical Society.*

The added eleven days would also have been involved in his figuring. If Henry had been born after February 18, his new birthday would have been in March, as Harry's earlier notation suggests. Then there is the issue of birth year: "next February" suggests that his son was born well before New Year's Day according to the old calendar, so—as in the case of George Washington—the year of his birth changed with the calendar in 1752. It's no wonder Frankland was confused about the age of his son.

The only thing left for an equally confused researcher reading Frankland's handwritten notes two and a half centuries later was to theorize on the basis of the visual evidence.

In the August notation, Harry's firm handwriting indicates that he is positive about Sally McClester's age. He gives the date of March 25. If she had been born on or after the Julian New Year's Day, her birth year would not change. His almost parenthetical jotting about Henry is of a different character. The first line ends abruptly with those strange slash marks after the words: "Henry Cromwell was 17." Underneath this statement, Frankland pens the abbreviation "Mar." in much smaller script than the rest of the entry. It is almost the graphic equivalent of a whispered question. Was he thinking "March"? There is no date and no year. The October entry is in a firm hand. The month, "February," is spelled out.

Frankland had a fascination with the natural sciences and astronomy. But was he beyond making a simple mathematical mistake?

The left-hand pages of his journal are a compendium of personal activity, axioms, aphorisms, botanical notes and household hints. On the right-hand pages he keeps a strict accounting of his expenditures, down to the cost of a quart of milk. That doesn't sound like a man who can't figure out the date of his son's birth.

The context is also important. Less than a year before these entries were made, Harry Frankland had been buried alive in the Lisbon earthquake. Such a traumatic experience would have rattled the memory of much stronger men.

I decided to go with Harry's more positive October entry, assuming that he had performed a simple calculation using the Gregorian years: 1757-1741=16. Careful historians would "double date," writing February 1740/1 to note the year of Henry's birth in both calendars. By Harry's calculations, Sally was born in 1740 in both calendars; Henry was born in 1740 Julian and 1741 Gregorian. More importantly, was Harry in England when Henry was conceived or in Boston?

Harry's May 19, 1740 letter to the Duke of Newcastle gives some indication of his state of mind at the time. He is eager to leave America, even pressuring a "Mr. White" to intercede for him in negotiations to rent an estate in Nottinghamshire. He is clearly bored, saying that he "begins to grow sick of the people." This sounds like a twenty-four-year-old man who misses his jolly companions in England, along with the women available there.

We know from the October 1739 *Boston Gazette* article that Harry was selling European and East Indian goods from a local warehouse. Ashley Bowen told us that in 1743, Harry was both king's collector and a Boston merchant trading in dried cod, which he most certainly had been buying in Marblehead.

Counting backward from Henry's birth month, his conception would have occurred in May 1740 in both calendars. This conception date would mean that Harry and Agnes met in the spring of 1740, when she was fourteen years old, directly contradicting the age of sixteen given in virtually every version of the legend.

Agnes's age at their meeting has traditionally been calculated from the date of the work in progress at Gale's Head. However, there are several accounts that do not link her encounter with Frankland to construction of the fort. These usually refer to "some business" connected to his collectorship.

Short of DNA testing or discovery of new primary evidence, we may never know the true identity of Henry Cromwell's mother. But Agnes Surriage is clearly the most logical candidate. Marblehead may well have a new claim to fame: "The Birthplace of Oliver Cromwell's Great-Great-Great-Grandson's Mother."

CHAPTER 13

The World Turned Upside Down

If buttercups buzz'd after the bee,
If boats were on land, churches on sea,
If ponies rode men and if grass ate the cows,
And cats should be chased into holes by the mouse,
If the mamas sold their babies
To the gypsies for half a crown;
If summer were spring and the other way round,
Then all the world would be upside down.
—from "Blackletter Ballad," originally written in 1643 as a protest against the ending of all the favorite English Christmas traditions as a result of Oliver Cromwell's victory at the Battle of Naseby. Some historians claim that the British army played it as it surrendered at Yorktown in 1781

With reliable primary evidence and rudimentary calculations pointing to the fact that she was the mother of Harry's child, I decided to proceed on the assumption that her family would recognize Agnes's condition in late August or early September 1740—near the time of George Whitefield's evangelical sermon.

What happened after that? Where and when was Henry Cromwell born? Where and when did Agnes's schooling begin? Who took care of the boy?

The first logical objective would be to get Agnes out of sight.

In dealing with Frankland's legendary removal of Agnes from Marblehead (more than two years after my theoretical calculation of their meeting), the literature presents various descriptions coined according to the popular mores of the era in which they were written:

> *Perhaps in the autumn of the same year* [1742]*...he sought, and gained permission of her parents...to remove her to Boston to be educated.*
> —*Nason, 1865*

> *One day in the autumn of 1742 a coach and four drove up to the door of the Inn...the guest was Sir Harry Frankland*[77]*...A short time after, when Frankland again visited the town...seeking her parents, he obtained their permission to remove her to Boston, where she was permitted to enjoy the best educational advantages.*
> —*Roads, 1880*

> *During the summer* [of 1742] *Sir Harry Frankland, then Collector of Boston, made a business visit to Marblehead...after his attention was attracted to* [Agnes] *Frankland, a young man of about twenty-six years, called her to his side, and made some kindly enquiries in relation to her parents...He sought and gained permission of her parents to remove her to Boston to be educated.*
> —*Sanborn, 1904*

> *It was not long before he had convinced her parents...and her minister, Dr. Edward Holyoke,*[78] *that he would like to educate her and take her to Boston as his ward.*
> —*Lord and Gamage, 1972*

These accounts are based on hearsay associated with the well-worn legend. With one exception, they link the encounter between Harry and Agnes to the fort's renovation in 1742. Virtually all of the essential details—the time of their meeting, her departure for Boston and the reason for leaving Marblehead—have been handed down from verbal history collected in the nineteenth century by Oliver Wendell Holmes and Elias Nason, clouded by the haze of four generations.

If my conclusions are correct, Agnes's identity as Henry's mother is one of the best-kept secrets of the eighteenth century. The only hints of it come from England: the Payne-Gallwey letter and the Yorkshire pedigree, both of which are secondary sources, created without access to Harry's journal.

I searched for a letter, a journal entry or a newspaper article for primary confirmation on this side of the Atlantic but found none. Although many well-born men fathered natural children, Harry was a member of an old and established family. His child would carry the bloodline of Oliver Cromwell. This means that there have been many people with reason to hide the fact of Agnes's lowborn identity and tender age from posterity.

If her pregnancy became general knowledge in Marblehead, both Agnes and Harry could have been prosecuted for fornication in the court at Salem. As opposed to a more relaxed attitude in cosmopolitan London, feelings about issues of sexual conduct in the colonies were not as liberal. According to Richard Godbeer, author of *Sexual Revolution in Early America*: "The prosecution of men and women for 'fornication' and of married couples whose firstborn were conceived prior to their formal entry into wedlock accounted for just over half (53%) of all criminal prosecutions in Essex County, Massachusetts between 1700 and 1785."

But first there would have to be evidence and witnesses willing to testify.

While there was not much chance of Harry being hauled to court, he had much to fear. His reputation would suffer when word of his indiscretion hit the salons of Boston, not to mention the drawing rooms of London, Yorkshire and Nottingham. His position as the heir-presumptive to the Frankland title, estate and fortune could be damaged. The clout of his connections with the Duke of Newcastle and the royal court would be seriously vitiated.

In Marblehead, talk of their daughter's pregnancy would have been a crushing blow to her family. Fishermen were known for a fierce clannish pride. The public stature of her lover would engender more *schadenfreude* than envy among the Surriages' neighbors.

Unless the situation was handled quickly and adroitly, the price Harry and the Surriage family would pay could be high indeed. Harry had both money and position. He would have put them to work keeping the matter under wraps and having Agnes removed from sight as soon as possible.

At the center of this maelstrom was a fourteen-year-old adolescent, confused and disoriented, with any fantasy she might have had about marrying a rich nobleman transformed into a nightmare. Her feelings of helplessness, guilt and fear must have been indescribable.

I believe Harry Frankland's journal—particularly his use of Agnes's niece as a benchmark for the date of Henry Cromwell's birth—hints at a possible scenario. By linking Henry Cromwell's age with that of Sally McClester in 1757 ("17 years of age next March"), Sir Harry associates Mary McClester with Henry's birth.

There is no mention of Mary's marriage in Second Church records and no listing for a McClester in Marblehead Vital Records, which leads me to believe that she could have been living somewhere other than Marblehead. If this were the case, Mary and her infant would have provided a safe haven for Agnes. Harry Frankland's robust assistance to the McClester family would be ensured, since the prevailing code of behavior made him responsible for the support of the boy[79] and his mother.

Agnes could then deliver the baby out of town and leave him under her sister's care to be raised with Sally. (This would explain why Henry Cromwell appeared at Hopkinton in 1752, accompanied by Mary and her children.) Those in Marblehead who asked about Agnes would be told that she was staying with Mary to help with her new baby. A year later, perhaps in the fall of 1742, when the legend traditionally begins, she would return home. Then, the story about Harry asking the Surriages' for permission to have her educated in Boston seems more plausible.

Agnes's whole world was turned upside down. She had experienced pregnancy, given birth and been separated from her baby. Before she had a chance to assimilate the impact of these traumas, she was swept from the dusty streets and rocky crags of Marblehead to Boston's busy byways; from the physical work of chopping wood, fetching water and dumping commodes into the ocean at the Fountain Inn to mind-bending lessons in reading, writing, embroidery, dancing and music.

There seems to be no record of where Agnes lived in Boston. The literature contains suggestions that Francis Shirley, wife of Frankland's "friend" Governor William Shirley, took her in. Though Shirley and Frankland were undoubtedly acquainted, there is little evidence that they were either friends or—as some versions of the legend have hinted—rivals for the post of collector. They belonged to different generations and came from different cultures: William Shirley was twenty-two years older than Harry. He studied law in England and immigrated to Boston with his family in 1731.

In 1738, Shirley was an unemployed Boston lawyer. From March 1736/7 through July 1738, his wife Francis waged an intense letter-writing campaign literally pleading with the Duke of Newcastle to get her husband a government job—any government job—in New England.[80] Her language was dramatic. On March 2, 1736/7, she wrote: "I am in great hopes (from your Grace's general character of goodness, compassion and readiness to make your great station a blessing to those below you) that you not lett [*sic*] Mr. Shirley and nine children sink in a foreign country."

This does not sound like a woman who would readily open the doors of the governor's mansion to a serving girl from Marblehead as a favor to the newly appointed king's collector.

In his introduction to *The Correspondence of William Shirley*, editor Charles Henry Lincoln writes that the Duke of Newcastle had promised the collectorship to Mrs. Shirley but given it to Frankland. This is doubtful, considering the duke's connection to the Whig power structure, which was driven by the British merchants' lobby. He would not have given a key trade position to Shirley, who had served as king's advocate in New England and was a Tory to the core. It is more likely that Jonathan Belcher's retirement as governor of Massachusetts in August 1741 gave Newcastle an opportunity to assuage the persistent Francis Shirley.[81]

Harry had every reason to keep his "ward" from the eyes and ears of Boston gentility. While Nason imagines her caught up in the elite social swirl of the wealthy merchants and political figures who made up Harry's Boston milieu, Agnes's speech and mannerisms—acquired from fourteen years' exposure to rough-hewn fishermen and codfish widows—could not have been ready for prime-time audiences.

Marbleheaders were clearly identified by their distinctive accent. Samuel Roads described Header speech patterns as "broad and quick." To capture an air of authenticity for his book, *Agnes Surriage*, Victorian writer Edwin Lassetter Byner researched the "peculiar old Marblehead dialect" by visiting the seaport and engaging a group of well-seasoned fishermen in conversation while a friend took notes.[82] John Greenleaf Whittier made a heroic attempt at Marblehead's version of the language in his poem about Captain Floyd Ireson, who was tarred and feathered by the women of Marblehead for refusing to aid a fishing ship caught in a storm:

> *Here's Flud Oirson, for his horrd horrt,*
> *Torr'd an' futherr'd an' corr'd in a corrt* [carried in a cart]
> *By th' women o' Morble'ead!*

Under the heavy accent of the day, according to Marblehead historian Samuel Roads,[83] "hardly a family…escaped with a correct pronunciation of its name." To Agnes, Harry's friend Robert Auchmuty might have become "Muster Orchmonky." Harry Frankland would have been among the first to admit that Agnes needed finishing.

Most sources agree that he sent her to the well-known private school of Peter Pelham, located near the customhouse. Pelham had been an engraver in London. He and his son—also named Peter—came to America in the 1730s. Pelham's curriculum included "Dancing, Writing, Reading, Painting upon Glass, and all sorts of Needle Work."[84]

Agnes was a stranger in a strange land. I could not help thinking of anthropologist Kalvero Oberg, who coined the phrase "culture shock" in 1954. Oberg defined this condition in terms of foreign travel, but his description has an uncanny resemblance to what a young, love-struck Agnes Surriage must have felt:

Honeymoon Phase—During this period the differences between the old and new culture are seen in a romantic light, wonderful and new.

Negotiation Phase—After some time (usually weeks), differences between the old and new culture become apparent and may create anxiety. This phase is often marked by mood swings caused by minor issues or without apparent reason. Depression is not uncommon.

Adjustment Phase—Again, after some time (usually 6–12 months), one grows accustomed to the new culture and develops routines. One knows what to expect in most situations and the host country no longer feels all that new. One becomes concerned with basic living again, and things become more "normal."

CHAPTER 14

A Desperate Uncle Thomas

While Harry was in Boston, the tides of his future continued to ebb and flow back in England.

Lady Dinah, wife of Sir Thomas Frankland, died on February 2, 1741/2, leaving him with two daughters and no male heir, increasing the possibility that the next oldest male heir—his nephew—would inherit his sumptuous estate and the title of baronet.

Having as his successor a young nephew whose reputation was already questionable would not have sat well with Sir Thomas Frankland. At fifty-six, he was a member of Parliament, member of the Board of Trade and highly connected in the court of George II. He needed a son—and soon.

It was not surprising, then, that Uncle Thomas quickly remarried, "shortly before 29 July 1743,"[85] according to *The Complete Baronage*. However, his choice of eighteen-year-old Sarah Moseley was probably just a little startling to the rest of the family.

Through the Internet, I accessed a document[86] that offers a glimpse of the new Lady Frankland's background. Warwickshire County Records contain a "conveyance by lease and release" dated January 1740/1 (Sarah was sixteen years old). The conveyance is to Sarah and her sister Jane from their Uncle John Mathew against his manor and a long list of properties held by tenant farmers. This meant that they would pay him an annuity (in this case £200) for a year. On the day after that year ended, Mathew was to "surrender to his nieces all his copyhold property."

So Uncle Thomas had married not only an outrageously young woman—he had also married an outrageously wealthy woman.

In May 1743, Fanny Russell, Harry Frankland's second cousin and woman of the bedchamber to Princess Amelia, wrote the following court gossip in a letter to her stepbrother, Lieutenant Colonel Charles Russell: "Sir Thomas and Lady Frankland were here last Thursday. They says [*sic*] she looks big, but I do not perceive it."

Two months later, on July 8, Fanny had a different observation: "Lady Frankland is certainly with child. Sir Thomas talks of going into his new house in a fortnight."

Sir Thomas Frankland, third baronet. *Photograph of a painting by Sir Godfrey Kneller. Payne-Gallwey photographs. Courtesy of the Massachusetts Historical Society.*

I found these letters in a special report, "Presented to Both Houses of Parliament by Command of Her Majesty," compiled in 1900. The authority of this document is important because Fanny's statement about Lady Frankland being "with child" on July 8 means that Sarah had conceived several months before her marriage on July 29. If *The Complete Baronage* date for his marriage is correct, then Sir Thomas did indeed father a son out of wedlock—two years after the birth of Henry Cromwell.

Colonel Russell's reply on August 23 may have reflected the sentiments of both the Frankland and Russell sides of the family: "I suppose in your next I shall hear of Lady Frankland having a boy or a girl; I must confess I hope it won't live." Obviously he didn't know that Sir Thomas's heir died on August 7, 1743—before he could be given a name.

A little over a year later, Colonel Russell penned another comment about Sarah that would become more accurate than he could have possibly imagined: "Lady Frankland has bedevil'd Sir Thomas and he is an old superannuated fool."

CHAPTER 15

Agnes off the Radar Screen

Iquickly learned that a paper trail for an obscure Marblehead fisherman's daughter born in 1726 is virtually nonexistent. Between the First Church record of her baptism and Sir Harry Frankland's will in 1768, I could find no official or contemporary document (with the exception of Harry's diary) mentioning Agnes Surriage. Her "adoption" as Harry Frankland's ward, departure from Marblehead to Boston and schooling can only be assumed from secondary information.

To cover the period of her life from 1741 to 1747, I harvested primary information from Boston newspapers and Frankland family correspondence documenting three crucial events that would have affected Agnes.

1743: A TRIUMPHANT CAPTAIN FRANKLAND RETURNS TO BOSTON

Sir Thomas Frankland wasn't the only member of the family to be married in 1743. On May 27 of that year, Harry's younger brother, Captain Thomas Frankland, wed the eighteen-year-old Sarah Rhett, daughter of a wealthy Charleston, South Carolina judge.

At the age of twenty-four, Captain Frankland had won fame and fortune through a brilliant naval career. He was commissioned as a lieutenant in 1737. By July 1740, he had been promoted to the command of the *Rose* frigate, with twenty-four guns. He was sent to the Bahamas, patrolling the coast of Florida and Carolina to seize Spanish and French privateers.

Thomas proved to be an aggressive and merciless commander. On June 20, 1743, the *Boston Post* carried this lively description of an eight-hour battle between the *Rose* and two Spanish privateers:

> *The gallant and vigilant Capt. Frankland, Commander of his majesty's Ship* Rose, *met and had a very smart engagement with two Spanish Privateers, a large Schooner of 16 Carriage (cannons) and as many swivel guns, with 140 men, and a sloop of 10 carriage, with 80 men. The Engagement lasted from about 4 O'clock in the Morning till Noon, when the Schooner sunk and all the men perished, which made a noble Dinner for such Fish as love Spanish carcasses. The Sloop ran aground at the Metanzes, and had the abundance of her men killed by the* Rose, *as they endeavored to get to shore.*

On July 29, 1743, the perennial family correspondent, Fanny Russell, sounds as though she can hardly wait to tell her stepbrother about the young lady "Tommy" had married: "Sir Thomas Frankland has had a letter from his nephew, Tommy Frankland, saying that he hopes to get his station at Boston, since his brother Harry has no thoughts of coming to England, and announcing his marriage to a young lady of eighteen, a very pretty woman."

And again on August 19: "The Lightfoots have had a letter from their Brother Bob, who tells them that Tommy Frankland was come there with his wife, and that she could sing and play and was quite an accomplished young lady."

In his reply, Lieutenant Colonel Russell offers us a rare hint of the contrast between the two brothers: "I'm told of more prizes that Capt. Frankland has taken; that he had a present of a piece of plate made him with the thanks of the merchants trading to Carolina[87] for the great services he has done in protecting their trade. I hope poor Harry is well."

With a military man's respect for rank, Thomas becomes "Captain Frankland" in his cousin's letter, but Harry is not only an afterthought—he is "poor Harry." Is this a reference to his health? Harry is twenty-seven. The gout that will trouble him later in life has probably not appeared. His coveted royal appointment is netting him more income than Governor Shirley. Keeping in mind that he was responding to Fanny's comments about Thomas's marriage, one wonders if Russell's condescension is a reference to Harry's personal life.

On August 22, 1743, the *Boston Evening Post* celebrated the entry of the *Rose* into Boston Harbor with a mawkish poem dedicated to Harry's brother, which contained lines like:

We see thee, Frankland, dreadful o'er the main,
Not terrible to children, but to Spain.
With thee, thy dawning beams of glory play,
And triumph in the prospect of the day.

I was curious to learn if the "brother Bob" Lightfoot in Fanny's letter was Harry's business partner. The Colonial Society of Massachusetts has documents that report the sale of an Attleboro, Massachusetts ironworks to a Judge Robert Lightfoot, a "merchant in Boston," in 1742. The *Memoirs of the Rhode Island Bar* state that Judge Robert Lightfoot was born in London in 1716 (he was the same age as Harry), educated at Oxford and had two sisters residing in London[88] (no doubt "the Lightfoots" in Fanny's letter).

Added to the *Boston Post* poem, Fanny's letter suggests that Captain Thomas Frankland had brought the *Rose* into Boston with his bride aboard, in which case he would undoubtedly have visited Harry. In his romantic Victorian style, biographer Nason visualizes the "gallant commander interchanging words with the beautiful Agnes Surriage, now fresh with the bloom of seventeen summers."[89]

If the Lightfoot visit took place in Boston, it meant that Harry—and possibly Agnes—had the pleasure of meeting Sarah Rhett. Imagine a foursome consisting of Captain Thomas, his eighteen-year old southern belle, Harry and Agnes. How this meeting affected a seventeen-year-old fisherman's daughter from Marblehead—if she was present—can only be conjecture.

1745: HARRY FRANKLAND BUYS MARY SURRIAGE'S SHARE OF THE "BROWN TRACT"

The Maine Historical Society contains a "Deed of Mrs. Mary Surriage, Marblehead, Massachusetts to Henry Frankland, Boston, Land at Muscongus." As the granddaughter of John Brown, Mary had inherited one-seventh of a tract he purchased from Samoset, a Native American, in 1625. Here is more evidence that Agnes is the mother of Harry's child. He felt such a strong obligation to the Surriage family that he paid her mother fifty pounds—half a year's salary—for a piece of land he had never seen and would never use or sell.

But the irony of the transaction is what Harry never knew. In reading John Brown's biography in *The General Dictionary of Maine and New Hampshire,*

I discovered that the Brown Tract was not what it appeared to be: "John Brown Pemaquid, whose name is a thousand times in print, chiefly because of a forged Indian deed antedated nearly a century."

A group of Brown descendants, using their knowledge of early settlers and places in the Pemaquid/Bristol area, had written the Samoset deed in the second decade of the eighteenth century and passed it off as a 1625 original until the deception was discovered one hundred years later.

1747: HARRY INHERITS THE FRANKLAND BARONETCY

Uncle Thomas died on April 23, 1747. Harry, his eldest male descendant, became heir to the Frankland baronetcy and estate. With his title, Sir Charles Henry Frankland gained new stature among the choice members of Boston society and the congregation of King's Chapel, where he was an active member. By this time—five years after her relocation from Marblehead—Agnes was living with Harry.

While in London "it was commonplace for respectable men to keep mistresses and to walk out in public with them,"[90] the more conservative Boston elite of the 1740s was not ready for Sir Charles to attend social functions, not to mention church services, with his twenty-one-year-old "ward."

No doubt Agnes had adapted to her surroundings. But the snide remarks and dark glances could not help but take their toll on a twenty-one-year-old woman, especially if there were rumors that she had been ripped out of adolescence by an unexpected pregnancy.

CHAPTER 16

A Little Bit of
Old England

R oger Price was born the son of an English country vicar during
the last decade of the seventeenth century. Throughout his life,
Price identified with his family's casual, gentrified lifestyle. In 1728,
he became rector of King's Chapel in Boston, an urban church with a
culture diametrically opposed to that of his bucolic background. Two
years later, the Anglican hierarchy in England appointed him commissary
(bishop's representative in the colonies) as well. But his frequent clashes
with a series of assistant ministers and an inflexible congregation became
unbearable to a man who had been conditioned to the casual life of the
English countryside.[91]

Increasingly, the church power structure chafed at Price's style. The
comprehensive Annals of King's Chapel records that "Mr. Price had the
habits of an English gentleman and country rector and that these were
widely divergent from New England ways." On October 20, 1733, King's
Chapel vestrymen complained that Price caused a "very serious accident"
by leaving his chaise unattended in an alley with his horse, "a very unruly
one" still in harness. The horse bolted, running over an older woman and
killing her, "and a child was much hurt at the same time."

Seeking a more compatible environment, Commissary Price acquired four
hundred acres in Hopkinton, a new settlement twenty-six miles northwest
of Boston, in 1736. On this land, he built a church. His strategy was to
convince the Society for the Propagation of the Gospel in Foreign Parts to
establish a mission in Hopkinton, where he could retire in bucolic comfort.

Fox Hunt at Mount Vernon—the start. *Courtesy of Fraunces Tavern® Museum, New York City.*

A royal charter established the Society for the Propagation of the Gospel in 1701. Still in existence, its original mission was to "ensure that sufficient mainteynance [*sic*] be provided for an orthodox clergy to live amongst the colonists and that such other provision be made as may be necessary for the propagation of the gospel in those parts."[92] (In other words, to spread the word among the natives.)

As soon as he landed in Boston, Harry Frankland had become a prominent member of King's Chapel. The church's wooden edifice was in disrepair, and in 1741, Frankland donated fifty pounds sterling toward its restoration. Harry's status in the landed gentry no doubt impressed Commissary Price. The two men became close friends.

Hopkinton offered Harry and Agnes an escape from the self-righteous indignation of Boston society. In 1751, the collector purchased 426 acres of land in Hopkinton along the southwestern slope of a hill the locals called Mount Magunco.

From the *Annals*:

> *Through the years 1743–44 and 1746–54,* [Charles Henry Frankland] *was elected annually a member of the Vestry of King's*

Chapel, but the displeasure with which his mode of life was regarded in Boston, outside the circle of those who made ample allowance for courtly English fashions—notwithstanding the Baronetcy which devolved upon him in 1747—caused him to remove to the country estate which he had purchased amid that charming landscape.

Harry and Agnes wasted no time leaving Boston. While their new mansion was being built, they moved into the vacant home of Commissary Price, who had retired to England. Harry spared no expense. The Frankland estate in Hopkinton was lush by the standards of any century.[93]

The manor house was three full floors high, with a one-hundred-foot frontage. Its square entrance hall opened to a double staircase. On the first floor were a large music room, a tremendous kitchen and a dining hall capable of seating fifty people at table. The second floor had bedrooms for the family and guests, while a third floor contained servants' quarters. The wall coverings were "not common hanglings [*sic*],"[94] suggesting hand-painted wallpaper similar to that preserved in Marblehead's Lee Mansion.

Harry was once again at home among his plants. In addition to rare species for his formal gardens, he imported boxwood hedges, buckthorn and lilacs.

As late as 1937, the Historic American Buildings Survey[95] described "Sir Henry Frankland Place" with an upper terrace, where the original house had stood, carved into the hillside and gardens on three large terraces at the rear. In addition, the house and grounds were surrounded with deep woods and fields, ideal for an eighteenth-century English gentleman's fox hunting. Numerous ponds and the convergence of the Charles, Concord and Fresh Springs Rivers accorded excellent fishing.

Elias Nason, whose family owned the house before it burned down in 1858, says there were traces of a large barn, a granary and 130 acres of farmland.

The mansion was finished during the summer of 1752. From Nason and Hopkinton records, it is clear that Henry Cromwell, now age eleven, moved in with Harry and Agnes. Later entries in Sir Harry's journal indicate that Agnes's sister—now Mary Swain—and her children also joined them.

The warrant for Hopkinton's town meeting held on February 18, 1753, contained an article asking "to see whether the town will grant the [petition] of Sir Charles Henry Frankland with regard to turning a road that passes though his land." This was a swath that Harry had cut from his mansion for access to the town of Hopkinton. It is known today as Frankland Street.

The couple had no trouble gaining acceptance in their new community, as reported in the *Annals*: "The center of the gay life in this arcadia was Charles Henry Frankland, a descendent of Oliver Cromwell, and heir presumptive to the family baronetcy with estates at Thirkleby and Mattersey—a young man of fortune and education."

For the first fourteen years of her life, Agnes had lived in a humble fisherman's cottage. At home, she would have spent most of her time in one room, the family "keeping room," comprising the entire downstairs of the house. This room literally "kept" the family together. Within its oak beams and pine paneling, they cooked in a huge fireplace, ate at their pine trestle table, read the Bible and slept by the fire on cold nights.

Imagine a handsome, twenty-six-year-old Agnes, dressed in London's finest fashion, standing in the enormous hallway for the first time, her gaze slowly drifting up the double staircase. Did she reflect back on that sparse home in Marblehead? Or did her thoughts reach beyond the beauty of these new surroundings to the realization that for the first time the three of them—Agnes, her son and the man she loved—were under the same roof? Perhaps then her Marblehead pragmatism would have taken her straight to the harsh reality: they were under the same roof but not as a family.

PART III
Vindication

CHAPTER 17

A Lawsuit…and a Marriage

Harry and Agnes's idyll would last for less than two years. May 1754 found Sir Charles Henry Frankland in London at Westminster Hall. He was appearing before the Court of the King's Bench as plaintiff in litigation against "the Lady of the late Sir Thomas," his Aunt Sarah, who was eleven years his junior.

When Uncle Thomas died in 1747, Lady Frankland produced a will that surprised and enraged every surviving relative save one: his widow. "I give and bequeath unto my dear and loving wife Dame Sarah Frankland all my jewels, plate, pictures, coaches, horses, linen, books, household goods, and all my goods, chattels, and all my personal estate whatsoever to hold and enjoy for her own proper use and benefit."[96]

Sarah got everything except the baronetcy, from the mansion and farms down to the horses and their hay. In addition, the will specified that any monies resulting from the sale of the estate be given to "said dear and loving wife Dame Sarah Frankland, her heirs, administrators and assigns." In sum, the family had lost the Frankland land grant forever.

This was enough to activate Sir Charles Henry Frankland, king's collector and bearer of the family escutcheon. He left for England almost immediately, taking Agnes with him.

Frankland's biographer, Elias Nason, quotes the *Gentleman's Magazine* 24 (July 1754), which neatly summed up the trial:

Monday, May 20, 1754
A case between Sir Harry Frankland, plaintiff, and the Lady of the late
Sir Thomas, defendant was tried in the Court of Kings Bench by a special
jury; the subject of the litigation was a will of Sir Thomas suspected to be
made when he was not of sound mind, and it appeared that he had made
3: one in 1741, another in 1744 and the third in 1746.

In the first, only a slender provision was made for his lady, by the second,
the family estate in Yorkshire of £2500 per annum was given her for life.
And by the third, the whole estate, both real and personal was left to be
disposed of, at her discretion, without any provision for the heirs at law.

The jury, after having withdrawn for about an hour and a half, set aside
the last and confirmed the second.

"Transcribed from a column
in Penaverde Portugal."
Photo by the author from journal
courtesy of the Massachusetts
Historical Society.

In its "Historical Chronicle" for the July issue, *Gentleman's* gives us an amusing endnote: "On a hearing before the Lord Chancellor, between Sir Henry Frankland, Bart. plaintiff, and Lady Frankland, defendant, in relation to the costs of the suit determined in May last, his lordship was pleased to decree, that the lady should pay all costs, both at common law and at Chancery."

For Harry, it would be a hollow victory. Sarah still owned Thirkleby for life, and—as it turned out—she outlived him.

Agnes's presence in London had a chilling effect on his relatives. As the holder of the baronetcy, Harry was expected to behave with decorum suitable to his position. To say the least, taking a common fisherman's daughter for a mistress and having the gall to introduce her into the family circle was unacceptable.

There can be no doubt that both Harry and Agnes were feeling the pressure. After thirteen years together, they had proved their love for each other. Now that bond was being tested as never before. It is one thing to sit in Boston and imagine the reaction to Agnes in London and quite another to be there experiencing the family's undiluted scorn in person.

Sir Charles Henry Frankland's journal, housed in the Massachusetts Historical Society, begins in Lisbon on March 17, 1755. Harry tends to include marginal notes of relevant personal details, For example, this ironically prescient note: "Monday, March 24, overturned in chaise."

The left-hand page for April 21 contains this entry:

Transcribed from a stone pillar at Penneverde in Portugal.

SOLUTIS	*SALVOS IRE,*
VOTIS	*SUSCEPTIS*
SALVOS	*VOTIS SAL*
REDIRE	*VOS IRE*
SALVOS	*REDIRE* [1543]

(Translation: *Left*: "Our vows performed we go in peace"; *Right*: "Our vows made, we go in peace")

In *A Visit to Portugal and Madeira*, written by Lady Emmeline Stuart-Wortley in 1854, I found this description of the Catholic Chapel in Pena Verde:

> *The chapel is built on a terrace. There is an inscription over the door; another on a little pillar over the portico; and on each side of the door there are also inscriptions:*

On the right side	*And on the left side*
Solutis votes	*Salvos ire*
Salvos redire	*Susceptis votes*
Salvos redire	*Salvos ire 1543*

Lady Emmeline and Harry are describing the same inscription.

The right-hand page opposite Harry's entry about the pillar is headed: "17th Week 1755 Acc [Accounts]." For accounting purposes, weeks began on January 1, 1755, which was a Wednesday—the beginning of the seventeenth week began with April 21. This page lists various expenses, including the baker, wig maker and postage, followed by some notes on the architecture in Portugal and, at the bottom: "According to records of the Second Church in Marblehead, my wife was baptized by the Reverend

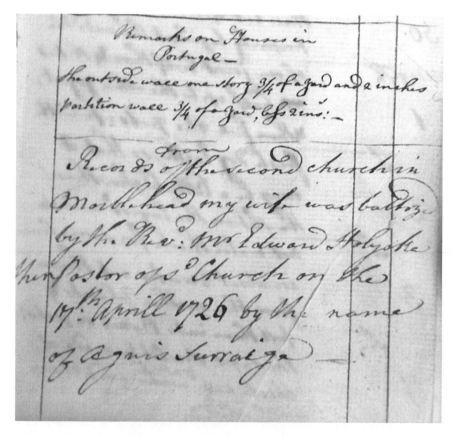

"My wife was baptized by Mr. Edward Holyoke." *Photo by the author from journal courtesy of the Massachusetts Historical Society.*

Mr. Edward Holyoke, then pastor of Church on the 17th April 1726 by the name of Agnis Surriage."

Here is a reference to Agnes as his wife, dated six months before the earthquake.

But why would an upstanding Church of England communicant marry out of his faith? And why would a Catholic priest in a country known for its conservative theocracy—indeed, the seat of the Spanish Inquisition—marry two Protestants?

In the Church of England, a baronet with Harry's prominent public stature would be required to have an elaborate formal wedding ceremony. Under the present circumstances, Harry could easily envision the humiliation of a wedding with none of the invited relatives attending. Engaging an Anglican minister in Portugal would have generated conversation among the British Anglican community. All the evidence I could find indicates that while Harry was socially outgoing, he remained secretive about his personal life. He would have wanted to control where and when this marriage was announced.

It is also conceivable that the priest of a poor parish in a small village on the outskirts of Lisbon could be convinced to perform such a profane marriage for the kind of donation Harry would be able to offer.

Ralph Payne-Gallwey, who supplied the Yorkshire Archaeological Society with much family history in the first decade of the twentieth century, did not have access to the journal, but in his notes accompanying a letter to the *London Spectator*[97] he offers his own reasons for believing that Sir Harry and Agnes were married before the earthquake. First, he quotes a letter by Frederick Meinhart Frankland (Harry's uncle) to his stepdaughter, the countess of Talbot: "13 July 1755...I commend your prudence about Sir Harry and am most sorry there is occasion for it."

Payne-Gallwey interprets this to be a reference to the countess's treatment of Sir Harry and Agnes, "who," he says, "—to the scandal of the family, were living together."

Then he cites a line from Uncle Frederick's personal journal a month later: "August 16, 1755: On Sunday last Sir Harry and Lady Frankland dined with me."

From this passage, Payne-Gallwey concludes: "It is evident that on August 16 1755 Sir Harry and Agnes Surriage were man and wife, or Frederick, his uncle, would never have received them in his house to dinner, or called Agnes Lady Frankland! It is probable, therefore, that the marriage took place between the dates of the two extracts."

He adds that there was no other Lady Frankland alive in 1755, except Uncle Thomas's widow, the defendant in Harry's lawsuit.

Harry and Agnes arrived back in England from Lisbon on June 16, 1755. Harry's journal has a single entry for July and another for August 1755. (Throughout his journal, he inserts aphorisms as if speaking to himself.)

> *July 6—Came to my house in Claris street (London). Proceed not to speak, or to act, before thou hast weighed the words and examined the tendency of every step thou shalt take.*
>
> *Terrify not thy soul with vain fears; neither let thy heart sink within thee from the phantoms of imagination.*

Harry is mulling over a disclosure of some kind. Usually he is careful to make an entry whenever they move from one location to another. The absence of such a note during this stay in England leads me to believe that they lived in London throughout July and August. Perhaps he told a few select members of the family about their marriage sometime between Frederick Frankland's letter to the countess of Talbot and the journal note.

Agnes was now twenty-nine—fourteen years and 3,250 miles from Marblehead. Her life with Harry had transformed her from an adolescent girl into a woman who combined worldly knowledge with the self-reliance of her codfish widow predecessors. She was becoming a matron, the mother of a son who ostensibly had been raised with her sister's children for eleven years. Her life was in bits and pieces: a little mistress, a phantom slice of wife, a smattering of motherhood. She stood alone amid the gentrified society in which she moved, but her new stature as Harry's wife undoubtedly put Agnes on more firm ground.

She was now officially Lady Agnes Frankland.

CHAPTER 18

Why Lisbon?

How did it happen that Sir Charles and Lady Agnes Frankland wound up at the epicenter of the eighteenth century's preeminent catastrophe, the Lisbon earthquake of 1755?

After losing Thirkleby and being soundly rebuffed by the Frankland relatives, the logical next step for Sir Harry would have been to make a quick exit back to Boston, where he still held the position of collector. Instead, he and Agnes turned up in Portugal. Why?

This led me to the search for a possible Frankland/Lisbon connection. Not surprisingly, what I found involves both money and politics. In 1693, Portugal discovered the world's richest cache of gold in Brazil, to be followed—thirty-five years later—by a mother lode of diamonds.

Harry's link was forged in 1654, well before Portugal's windfall. His shrewd ancestor, Oliver Cromwell, made a treaty giving military assistance to Portugal, which was then at war with Spain. In return, he got the Portuguese to grant British merchants special trading rights. The result was the British factory, a trading center and British community in Lisbon.

Over the years that followed, the factory negotiated with the Portuguese government for increased privileges. London put additional pressure on the Portuguese authorities when necessary. By 1739, the factory's high-powered dealing, backed by the muscle of the British Empire, had created a trade imbalance that reduced Portugal to little more than England's cash cow.

The Portuguese realized they needed to level the playing field. To accomplish this, they sent their heaviest hitter to London: a rising star of the

Lisbon court, whose towering physique and jaw-breaking name (Sebastiao Jose de Carvalho e Melo) commanded immediate attention.

His partner in the negotiations was none other than Thomas Pelham Holles, Duke of Newcastle, who had appointed Harry collector in 1741. Carvalho was successful in achieving better conditions for Portuguese merchants and some restrictions on the British merchant fleet. By 1754, he had become secretary of state. In England, Newcastle had risen to the post of prime minister.

So when Sir Harry went to England for the trial, the most influential man in the British government was the one to whom he had once written, "If your Grace will honor me, with any Commands here, they shall be punctually obey'd."

Brazilian gold and diamonds had made Lisbon a dazzling mercantile center, "rich in its tremendous commercial importance," according to T.D. Kendrick, author of *The Lisbon Earthquake*. As such, it played a key role in British commerce. An urgent trade deal involving the British factory (or simply the need to have his own man on the scene) may well have caused Newcastle to dispatch Harry—whose father had been the governor of the factory at Bengal—to Lisbon for whatever service he could render.

CHAPTER 19

November 1, 1755

Primary research helped me transcend the dramatic earthquake accounts embedded in the legend. This is an extract from a letter by Sister Catherine Witham, a Bridgettine nun of Syon House, Lisbon, to her mother in England, dated January 27, 1755/6:[98]

> *Sir Henry Franklen* [sic] *an acquaintance of Mr. Killinghall was going in his shayz and perceived the houses to fall, he jump out an a house fell upon him, he gett out through some little hole and see a good many alive in a Nother street, he had Portugese to say Vene, that is come here, so saved them all, he left his shayz in the street broak, his servants and horses Killed.*

From the journal of Sir Charles Henry Frankland: "1755. Nov. During my residence in Portugal happened the great earthquake, on which day I was providentially saved. I was buried in the ruins. Francisco de Riberio lived in the house I was saved in at the time of the earthquake. Hope my providential escape will have a lasting good effect upon my mind."

Not quite the earthquake of the legend. Neither Sister Catherine nor Harry mentions Agnes appearing on the scene. Harry speaks of being "providentially saved" and his "providential escape" (not rescue), giving all the credit to God. Similarly, "he gett out through some little hole" does not conjure up pictures of muscular Portuguese fishermen, motivated by Agnes's gold shoe buckles, prying roof timbers from Harry's body.

The Lisbon earthquake, 1755, from a German engraving. *Courtesy of Wikimedia Commons.*

I searched for some shred of evidence that would verify the legend's assertion that Harry had a female companion who bit his arm as she died. My best guess is that it never happened.

There are several accounts of a room in the Hopkinton mansion to which Harry retired on each anniversary of the earthquake. There, he spent the day, praying and meditating. On the wall hung his torn, bloodstained jacket and bent sword. Spurred by the bloody jacket, succeeding generations could have added a dying companion to the legend for dramatic effect.

As to Agnes's whereabouts when the earthquake hit, we can only project dimly, for there is no record. Nothing in her life heretofore could have prepared her for the absolute chaos into which she was so suddenly plunged. While it is known that their house was destroyed, Agnes survived probably because a friend (or her pragmatic Marblehead nature) got her out of the house and onto the street, the safest place in an earthquake, where buildings are more likely to fall around you than on you.

A sea captain witnessing the disaster wrote: "If one went through the broad places of squares, [there is] nothing to be met with but people wringing their hands, and crying 'the world is at an end.'"

This twenty-nine-year-old woman had been steeped in the liberalism of Edward Holyoke, jolted by the Calvinist revivalism of the Great Awakening and then mellowed by the gentrified religion of Roger Price and the transplanted King's Chapel congregation in Hopkinton.

What kind of shock would she have felt when she saw and heard what another eyewitness described as "the sight of dead bodies, together with the shrieks and cries of those, who were half-buried in the ruins"?[99] To Agnes's eclectic theological mind, the Day of Judgment was surely at hand. Cutting through her terror would be immediate thoughts of her husband.

The earthquake began at 9:30 a.m. It lasted ten minutes, consisting of three distinct shocks about a minute apart. First there was a rumbling that some described as similar to distant traffic. After a pause, there came a huge shock lasting at least two minutes. In a roar of destruction, the roofs of churches fell on their congregations, houses disintegrated, shops crumbled and walls collapsed, burying thousands in the wreckage. The third shock was followed by an all-enveloping cloud of suffocating dust that filled the air, turning a sun-drenched fall day into a dark scene of horror.[100]

A firestorm erupted, ignited by the many church candles and cooking fires. To make matters worse, the fires were fanned by a strong wind that suddenly arose. The entire panorama of wreckage was soon in flames, with men, women and children trapped inside. "The whole city appeared in a blaze, which was so bright that I could easily see to read by it," wrote Reverend Charles Davy.[101]

From an English eyewitness: "Some attempt might perhaps have been made to subdue the conflagration, if the sea had not at the same time threatened to overwhelm Lisbon."[102]

The effect of the earthquake on the ocean and subsequently the Tangus River was enormous. Reverend Davy stood on the bank: "In an instant there appeared, at some small distance, a large body of water, rising as it were like a mountain. It came on foaming and roaring, and rushed towards the shore with such impetuosity, that we all immediately ran for our lives as fast as possible; many were actually swept away."

It is entirely possible that, as the legend has it, Agnes found Sir Harry during the initial phase of the disaster. Together, they would have sought safety from the chaos exploding around them. But there is no primary source of verification. What we do know is that somehow they found each other amid the mobs of hysterical people running, crawling and often clawing their way out of the destruction.

I picture Harry and Agnes, clothes torn, dirt on their faces—totally disheveled—standing together immersed in the carnage. Would they have found each other before or after Harry emerged from the wreckage and had the presence of mind to shout "vene" at a group of people? The details belong to history. But from eyewitness accounts, we can put together what they experienced in the days that followed.

An oft-quoted dialogue between the king and his secretary of state reflects the spirit of the recovery: "What is to be done to meet this infliction of Divine justice?" asked the king. "Bury the dead and feed the living," replied Carvalho, who then proceeded to take charge of the restoration of Lisbon in his characteristic dictatorial style. No matter how tyrannical his personality may have been, his decisive and sensible decisions during the crisis have earned him history's distinction as the hero of the Lisbon earthquake. A town is named for him. He is best known as the Duke of Pombal, a title bestowed on him in 1770.

As early as November 2, Sir Harry and Agnes would have witnessed carts and wheelbarrows filled with corpses being wheeled away from the ruins. The stench was horrific. Body removal was the essential first step to prevent a plague.

Looting began before the tremors were over. Carvalho ordered a summary death sentence rendered at the scene of the crime. The Franklands could not have missed the extra-high gallows with their grim hangings, erected so that all could be aware of the penalty.

As British subjects, Sir Harry and Agnes were well known to Abraham Casteres, Esq., envoy extraordinary to the king of Portugal. On November 6, five days after the first shock, he wrote a dispatch to the secretaries of state in England. The content and tone of this extract not only creates a picture of the situation but also provides an indication that he had seen the Franklands:

> *Most of the considerable families in our factory have already secured to themselves a passage to England by three or four London traders. They are preparing for their departure…We are in a day or two to have a meeting of our scattered factory at my house to consider what is best to be done in our present wretched circumstances…I must not forget to acquaint you that Sir Harry Frankland and his lady are safe and well.*

Nason quotes a letter from an English merchant published in the *Boston Gazette* on January 12, 1756: "Sir Harry Frankland, I am told, escaped miraculously…he and lady are now at Belem."

According to Kendrick,[103] there was a large encampment at Belem, to the west of Lisbon. Sir Harry and Agnes would have been living there in a tent or rough-hewn wooden building, waiting for a ship to return to England.

CHAPTER 20

Fallout

Reasonable estimates place the death toll of the earthquake at ten to fifteen thousand lives in Lisbon alone.[104] There was catastrophic destruction and heavy loss of life in the entire southwest corner of Portugal, as well as North Africa. Spain, Algiers and Gibraltar also suffered severe damage. Shocks were felt in the lead mines of Derbyshire, England, nine hundred miles away.

Essentially, the tremors decimated the city of Lisbon. They completely destroyed hundreds of houses and shops. The fire burned for nearly a week. It was responsible for great loss of wealth, including collections of art, plate, furniture and books. British and German traders alone lost goods that would be worth over $1 billion today.

Three tsunamis swept the six miles of river coast from Lisbon to the mouth of the Tangus, taking with them all of the light shore structures and many of the people who had come to the river as a place of safety. Ships were tossed and torn from their anchors as if in a violent storm. Many capsized with the crews aboard.

The earthquake shook more than the ground. It rattled the foundations of religious belief. From our sophisticated perch in the twenty-first century, it would be impossible to view this natural disaster as Harry, Agnes and the people of Lisbon did. We live in an age of unprecedented and immediate access to death and destruction. Vivid images and sounds of both human and natural violence are so much a part of our lives that we take them for granted. We trust our scientists to correlate the facts and objectively quantify natural disasters like floods, hurricanes and earthquakes.

Jean Jacques Rousseau. *Courtesy of Wikimedia Commons.*

Francois Marie Arouet. (Voltaire). *Portrait by Nicolas de Largilliere. Courtesy of Wikimedia Commons.*

Harry and Agnes had never seen carnage on such a large scale. The powerful emotions created by this experience would have made concerns about the Frankland family seem trivial by comparison. Their fear of God's fury had been realized in the stark reality of what they saw and heard. The words of Ezekiel had gained a new significance: "Then the Spirit lifted me up, and I heard behind me the voice of a great earthquake…it was the sound of the wings of the living creatures as they touched one another, and the sound of the wheels beside them, and the sound of a great earthquake."

We have no record of Agnes's reaction, but Harry expressed his thoughts in a section of his journal titled "At Sea" on December 23, 1755:[105]

> *We should endeavor to pacify the divine wrath by sorrow for past neglects and future conscientious discharge of our duty to God and our country.*
>
> *Natural calamities entirely proceed from the hand of God, and they are designed by providence as warnings to teach the inhabitants of the world righteousness.*

Almost without exception, the deeply religious people of Lisbon shared Harry's conviction that the earthquake was supernatural. They felt that the most important task before them was to pacify an angry deity with demonstrable expressions of penitence. Two large penitential processions took place: one a little over two weeks after the disaster and another in December. Stories of mystic healings, priests' bodies being found in a miraculous state of preservation and people emerging from the rubble unharmed were rampant.[106]

A popular belief system known as optimism prevailed in the Christian world. Propounded by the German philosopher Gottfried Wilhelm Leibniz, it held that "all is well." God created the world, and He is in charge. Everything that happens—good or bad—is for the best. "This is the best of all possible worlds."

But many Enlightenment intellectuals took an opposing view: the maker of the universe is indefinable. God observes human behavior without directly intervening in our lives. He gave us free will to make our own choices. The earthquake was not supernatural. It had natural causes.

Voltaire, a leading Enlightenment thinker and deist, wrote an epic poem a month after the Lisbon earthquake that he called "Poem on the Lisbon Disaster, or: An Examination of that Axiom 'All Is Well,'" in which he said:

> *Will you say, in seeing this mass of victims:*
> *"God is revenged, their death is the price for their crimes?"*

What crime, what error did these children
Crushed and bloody on their mothers' breasts, commit?
Did Lisbon, which is no more, have more vices
Than London and Paris immersed in their pleasures?
Lisbon is destroyed, and they dance in Paris!

In a caustic letter, Voltaire's archrival Rousseau, a proponent of optimism, replied:

All my complaints are…against your poem on the Lisbon disaster, because
I expected from it evidence more worthy of the humanity which apparently
inspired you to write it…Instead of the consolations that I expected, you
only vex me. It might be said that you fear that I don't feel my unhappiness
enough, and that you are trying to soothe me by proving that all is bad.

In *A History of Western Philosophy*, Bertrand Russell offers an interesting insight: "Rousseau, for his part saw no occasion to make such a fuss about the earthquake. It was quite a good thing that a certain number of people should get killed now and then."

CHAPTER 21

Life after Near Death

While the legend puts Harry and Agnes's first marriage in Belem immediately after the earthquake, Harry's journal leads us to believe that it actually took place six months earlier in Pena Verde. However, their legendary second ceremony aboard the ship from Lisbon to London in December 1755 probably did happen. The baronet would have wanted the union made official (and respectable) before seeing his family again.

Returning to England as Lady Frankland was Agnes's well-deserved vindication. If she had been instrumental in Sir Harry's "providential escape," she might well have received a warm—but reserved—welcome into the family.

Agnes's acceptance as the wife of a baronet left her with no illusions of grandeur. Throughout her life, she remained loyal to her heritage, providing lodging to her sister Mary and family, supporting her brothers and maintaining the self-assurance of a true Marblehead woman.

Harry's next journal entry is datelined "Don Gaston's House in Portugal, April 1756." It contains a list titled "Commissioners of Customs," with no accompanying comment. This may be significant, since the commissioners had control over mercantile activities in the colonies. In a sense, the absentee collector of customs was enumerating his superiors back in England. One of them, Sir John Evelyn, had been a member of Parliament with Uncle Thomas.

After returning to Boston in the summer of 1756, Frankland bought the house of William Clark, a wealthy Boston merchant. Its urban opulence made a perfect counterpart to Sir Harry's Hopkinton estate. Built in 1711, this twenty-six-room, solid brick mansion stood three stories high on Garden

Lady Frankland's fan. *Payne-Gallwey photographs. Courtesy of the Massachusetts Historical Society.*

The Clarke house, with Bunker Hill in the background. *Courtesy of Kellscraft Studio.*

Court Street at the base of Bunker Hill. The interior featured porcelain fireplaces with mantels of Italian marble and floors of inlaid pine and cedar.

His acquisition of a house in Boston would lead one to believe that Sir Harry intended to stay in New England for an extended period of time. In January 1757, he "Paid Johnny's schoolmistress £200." This was a reference to John McClester, a sign that Agnes's sister Mary and her children were still living in the Franklands' Hopkinton home.

In July 1757, nineteen years before the outbreak of the American Revolution, Harry felt it was important to note that "Mass Bay has on the alarm list 45,000 to bear arms. Training list 32,000." Also in July, he hired a French chef named Charles, and the *London Magazine* reported: "Sir Henry Frankland, Bart.

appointed consul general at Lisbon." Biographer Nason says that Harry sought the consulship because "Frankland, had, by his former residence in Portugal become well acquainted with its language and commercial regulations, and... his declining health demanded a milder clime."

In his journal for 1757, Harry lists a remedy for gout:

> *Receipt for the Gout—*
> *One pound of Rye Meal*
> *4oz of Yeast or Leaven*
> *2oz common salt*
> *Mix together with hot water into a poultice & applied to the bottom of the*
> *feet, where it will soon invite the disorder & carry it out between the toes.*

No doubt, Harry had gout and probably kidney stones. His penchant for visiting the Roman baths at Caldas in Portugal and later at Bath in England are clear indications. Benjamin Franklin, who lived substantially longer than Frankland, had the same commonly coexisting conditions. Both are painful and debilitating. They were prevalent in the eighteenth century mainly as a result of a diet heavy in red meat, rich food and wine.

But there may have been extenuating circumstances involved in Harry's Lisbon appointment. The dual role of West Indian merchant and Boston collector may have caught up with him. During Harry's two-year absence from the customhouse, the Frankland family's chief high-level sponsor, the Duke of Newcastle, had been forced into an uneasy co–prime minister relationship with his major political opponent, William Pitt. This may account for Samuel Adams Drake's comment in his 1876 book, *Landmarks of Boston*: "The Clark House was the residence of Sir Charles Henry Frankland, who was Collector of Boston under Governor Shirley. He was said to have been removed from this office for inattention to its duties."

A February 1758 journal note from Nottinghamshire indicates that Sir Harry and Lady Agnes sailed from Boston to England during the late fall or early winter of 1757. Harry's wandering thoughts turn to the genetic qualifications a lady must consider when choosing a husband: "No lady of distinction will marry any man unless he authentically makes it appear that his ancestors have been gentlemen and equally married for a succession of 16 generations."

According to an itinerary compiled by Ralph Payne-Gallwey from family records and correspondence, Harry and Agnes left London for Lisbon three months later, in June 1758.

CHAPTER 22

"…the Horrid Execution of the Marchioness Tavora"

A sentence from the biography on the back of Agnes's Chichester portrait caught my attention. "She also saw the horrid execution of the Marchioness Tavora." Who was Marchioness Tavora? Why was she executed? And how did Agnes happen to witness her execution? The answers hearken back to our old friend, Sebastiao Jose de Carvalho e Melo (aka the Duke of Pombal), and an event that took place shortly after Harry assumed his post.

In September 1758, there was an assassination attempt on King Joseph I. He received a wound in the arm as he was riding home from a liaison with his favorite mistress, Teresa Leonor, wife of Luis Bernardo, heir of the Tavora family.

At this point, Carvalho was Joseph's prime minister. The son of a country squire, he held a long-standing grudge against the old nobility and the Catholic Church, both of which despised him in turn.

From the February 1759 issue of the *Universal Magazine*: "As a kind of testimony of joy, when his Majesty recovered, the English Factory gave a ball, to which most of the Portuguese nobility were invited, and among the rest the Duke of Aveiro, his Duchess, and son." [107]

The newly arrived English consul general and his lady would have been among the guests. Imagine their reaction when

about one the next morning, the company broke up; and, as precedence is greatly minded in Portugal, nobody would presume to stir till the Duke was

Sebastiao Jose de Carvalho e Melo, the Duke of Pombal. *Courtesy of Wikimedia Commons.*

gone. But how were some of the company surprised, when, coming to the outward door soon after, in order to go home, they were denied permission; and, looking a little closer, saw all the avenues full of troops! The Duke of Aveiro, his Duchess, and son were arrested; and nobody was suffered to stir out till they had been safely lodged in prison.

Additionally seized and imprisoned was a virtual dynasty of nobility: the Marquis and Marchioness Tavora, their two sons, the Count of Antigua and his son-in-law and several other minor members of the king's court. Troops surrounded the colleges of the Jesuits. Ten priests were held as co-conspirators.

Carvalho wasted no time. He had an informer captured and tortured to reveal the names of the would-be assassins and the originators of the plot. All were given a common trial, in which the only evidence presented was the informer's confession (he had been executed before the trial), the weapon, which belonged to the Duke of Aveiro, and the assumption that the Tavoras would have disclosed the location of the king that night, since he was returning from a tryst with Teresa of Tavora (who was also arrested).

On Saturday, January 13, 1759, all of the defendants were slowly, brutally tortured and killed before a crowd estimated at seventy thousand on a twelve-foot-high stage in Belem, where Harry and Agnes were living. According to an eyewitness report, the fifty-year-old Marchioness Tavora, already suffering premature dementia, was beheaded to the shouts of the crowd. Her youngest son, described as a "youth of beautiful face, agreeable deportment, and amiable disposition," was escorted on stage between two friars and seated at a stake in the form of Saint Andrew's cross. After being strangled, his arms and legs were broken by eight blows from an executioner. The eldest son of the Marquis and Marchioness, age thirty-five, was then executed in the same manner.

After slow and painful executions of three family servants, the old Marquis of Tavora was tied to the wheel and had his bones broken while alive. He had arrived in an open cart with the Duke of Aveiro, who was forced to watch the marquis die. When he was freed from his bonds, the duke went to each of the preceding seven corpses, lifting the cloth that covered them. When he came to the young boy, he kneeled down, kissed the corpse and wept aloud. Tied to the cross, Aveiro first had his right arm broken, after which a herald proclaimed his crime above his shrieks, which "would have pierced the hardest heart." The executioner let him suffer in this manner for fifteen minutes before administering the coup de grâce.

The ninth to be murdered was Joseph Mascarenhas, who was also called Duke of Aveiro. Under the supposition that he had fired one of the blunderbusses at the king, his hands were "instantly chopped off." The executioner tied him to a cross, where he remained alive for an hour and a quarter, receiving eight strokes from the iron crowbar.

Like stagehands preparing for the last act, two men entered and prepared two stakes fitted with seats. These were for Aveiro's servants, who had confessed to shooting the king. One had escaped, so an effigy replaced him. The remaining servant was tied to the other stake, and all bodies were brought in and arranged around him. The corpses were covered with rosin "about an inch thick," having about the same effect as being doused with gasoline.

Then "the faggots were laid on, and fire set to that part of the stage where the bravo was fixed, who saw the clouds of smoke ascend around him with surprising resolution; not so much as moving or crying till the flames reached him; then his violent struggles and frightful cries were greatly affecting to the spectators." Both scaffold and bodies being consumed, the ashes were swept up and thrown into the Tangus.

Carvalho had the ground salted so that nothing would grow there.[108] He had settled two scores—his hatred of the aristocracy and the assassination attempt—with one horrific execution.

At the age of thirty-three, as the wife of a British official, Agnes had to watch all of this. It was an experience beyond the ken of a fisherman's daughter from Marblehead—one that had to create a new understanding of the human capability for cruelty, possibly adding an element of sobriety to her character.

On a happier occasion, the Franklands attended the wedding of the prince Don Pedro to his niece Donna Maria, princess of Brazil, on June 5, 1760.

Harry's journaling during this period is sometimes humorously eclectic, like this entry for June 15 of the same year: "The pope's nuncio ordered to leave the kingdom of Portugal. Rub knives and forks, guns, etc. with linseed oyl [sic] to preserve from rust." Casually mentioning a key political decision initiating the expulsion of the Jesuit order from Portugal followed by a household hint about rust proofing seems quixotic even for the baronet.

Harry's health was failing. After the royal wedding, he and Agnes spent the rest of their summers at Caldas de Rainha, where he took hot sulfur baths, observing: "The men's bath at Caldas is 46 palms (11.5 feet) long and will contain 60 persons at a time."

On December 8, 1760, Agnes unknowingly brushed with both her past and America's future. From the journal: "Col. Arnott, Mr. Lowrey and Burgoyne from Gibraltar dined with us." General John Burgoyne would command the British forces at the Battle of Saratoga in October 1777. Surrounded by rebels and peppered with musket fire, Burgoyne surrendered to General Horatio Gates. He and his troops were marched back to Boston by General John Glover's Marblehead Regiment. Burgoyne and Glover got to know each other during the trip and became friendly. Glover was born in Salem. His mother moved to Marblehead after being widowed in 1740, when Agnes was fourteen.

At this point in her life, Agnes was in the mainstream of the British diplomatic circle, riding, traveling the Portuguese countryside and entertaining their friends from the British factory.

Probably while he was soaking in the baths at Caldas, Harry began to ponder the relationship between Portugal and England, which, from this journal entry in 1761, might have been strained at the time: "The revenue of Portugal principally depends upon distant provinces which easily may be invaded by a nation powerful at sea, therefore it cannot be for the interest of Portugal to quarrel with Great Britain."

He has also left us a revealing diatribe, probably unleashed by the Seven Years' War, which was in progress: "The French, notwithstanding the deplorable and even despicable figure they make, talk in forms as haughty and imperious, as if they had everything in their power."

From August 7 to 11, 1761, Agnes and Sir Harry stayed at the small village of St. Martintro with five of their friends from the international set. This particular junket is noteworthy because there apparently was a precise scale in town, and all members of the party were weighed. Harry dutifully noted the statistics in his journal: Lady Frankland was 132 pounds; Sir Harry came in at 136. The average height for women in the eighteenth century was five feet, one half inches, indicating that thirty-five-year-old Agnes was getting a bit matronly.

During their summer at Caldas in 1762, Agnes suffered a "violent cold" with sore throat and "profuse sweats." Her doctor prescribed a gargle of "marsh mallows and figs boyled [sic] together with milk." This was followed by a strong purge. In November, she was purged again with a mixture of distilled sap from the flower ash plant and potassium sulfate.

Harry's entry on August 6, 1762, contains what may be another foreshadowing of his career status: "It is an error in politics, especially in regard to Portugal, to suffer any innovation, or infraction of treaty to pass unnoticed by the Public Minister abroad, or minister at home."

A year later, on August 17, 1763, the Franklands sailed from Lisbon for Falmouth aboard the *Hanover* packet. From there, they sailed for Boston.

CHAPTER 23

Bath and Beyond

In 1764, after a short period of shuttling back and forth between their homes in Boston and Hopkinton, Harry and Agnes returned to England, bound for the hot springs at Bath. Henry Cromwell (now a twenty-three-year-old lieutenant in the Royal Navy), Mary McClester and her son John accompanied them.

As far back as AD 50, when the Romans built a temple on the site of Bath, the waters were considered to have mystic healing power. By the eighteenth century, the area had been developed into a fashionable resort spa for the wealthy.

At this point, Harry's journal begins to sound like that of a gouty, grouchy old man. September 21, 1764: "I cannot suffer a man of low condition to exceed me in good manners." 1765: "The people of England are in general a set of hot headed fools; a parcel of senseless coxcombs who though perfectly able to examine the bottom of things, never judge farther than the surface."

In 1767, King George III replaced Harry with Sir John Hort, baronet of Castle Strange in the County of Middlesex, as consul general to Portugal

Sir Charles Henry Frankland, with Lady Agnes in attendance, died on January 11, 1768, at the age of fifty-one. He was buried near Bath in Weston Church. The plaque, "erected by his affectionate widow Agnes Lady Frankland," reads in part: "To the memory of Sir Charles Henry Frankland of Thirkleby in the county of York. Baronet, Consul-General for many years at Lisbon from whence he came in hopes of recovery from a bad state of health to Bath…he died 11th of January 1768 in the 52nd year of his age without issue and at his desire lies buried in this church."

The Roman Baths, Bath, England. *Photo by Andrew Dunn, courtesy of Wikimedia Commons.*

Harry's life was a panorama of sharp contrasts. From all indications, the environment of Bengal heavily influenced his childhood. For the first twelve years, native servants and nannies—women who were passive and tranquil by nature—would have influenced him. His love of horticulture could have had its origins amid the tropical flora. As he went through adolescence, he no doubt acquired from his peers the sense of entitlement that characterized young aristocrats of the era.

Frankland's family and station give credibility to Nason's assertion that his young manhood was spent in the company of notable personages such as Horace Walpole, son of the powerful Prime Minister Robert Walpole; Henry Fielding, raucous author of *Tom Jones*; and Phillip Stanhope, Earl of Chesterfield, whom Nason says resembled Harry "both in his manners and in his person." This is particularly ironic because Chesterfield is best known for letters of advice like the following, to his natural son (the offspring of a French governess): "Women are but children of a larger growth. A man of sense only trifles with them, plays with their humors and flatters them." Judging by the popular culture of the time and Harry's privileged status, these were his salad days of drinking and wenching.

Writing a journal is frequently the externalization of an internal dialogue. We can extrapolate Harry's thought processes to some extent from his choice of subjects. By the time he began his diary at age thirty-nine in 1755, he considered important—in addition to copious notes on gardening and personal expenses—moralistic aphorisms like: "The uneasiness thou feelest; the misfortunes thou bewailist; behold the root from which they spring, even thine own folly, thine own pride, thine own distempered fancy."

When he wrote this, he had suffered the scorn of both Boston and London, including censure by his family. Further, he had just lost the Frankland Yorkshire estate to an aunt who was but a year older than his mistress.

After his escape from a living tomb in Lisbon, he adopted an emphatic Calvinist tone: "It is certainly more agreeable to all our ideas of the majesties and perfections of God to consider Him as prevailing over the system of the world and employing the whole creation to execute the design either of mercy or of punishment."

Harry's journal of this era shows a latent compassion. He often includes "to the poor" in his itemization of expenses. He made a special note about witnessing a Portuguese tradition: "At the court to see the King wash the poor men's feet."

Whatever his initial intentions toward Agnes Surriage, his substantive support of Agnes's mother, as well as Mary McClester and her children, went well beyond what one might consider necessary to make amends for an unexpected pregnancy. From the time of her arrival in Boston as an adolescent until his death, his actions toward the Surriage family indicated a strong element of atonement.

Harry demonstrated complete acceptance of Agnes as his full partner in life by making her sole executrix of his estate. He left her all property in Boston and Hopkinton, plus a tax-free annuity of £400 per annum. He willed Henry Cromwell an annuity of £30, which, for reasons unknown, he increased to £100 in the last six months of his life. The annuities for Agnes and Henry were to come from the Mattersey estate in Nottinghamshire. Harry gave Agnes complete freedom to decide whether this should be accomplished by sale or mortgage.

The date of Harry's death plays a key role in debunking a popular misconception about Richard Potter, the son of Dina, a Hopkinton slave.

Richard became famous both here and in England as America's first African American magician and ventriloquist. Every Richard Potter biography I've ever read says Sir Harry Frankland fathered him. If so, it is the world's first case of posthumous paternity: Potter was born in 1783.

From the *Boston Chronicle*, June 13, 1768: "The Lady of the late Sir Harry Frankland came passenger with Captain Freeman [aboard the ship Juno] who arrived here last week from Bristol."

A letter[109] written by Henry Cromwell to Thomas Pelham, a distant cousin of Harry's and steadfast family friend, indicates that he returned to Boston with Agnes:

> *Boston 25 November 1768,*
> *Mr. Cromwell presents His most respectful Compliments to Mr. and Mrs. Pelham, hopes they and Family are well, and enjoy a perfect good state of Health…*
> *…Lady Frankland presents her Love and Compliments to Mr. and Mrs. Pelham, she had been extremely ill at times this summer with a violent pain in Her Stomack which she never had before she came to this country but is pretty well at present.*

Also in 1768, Sir Thomas Frankland, heir to the family baronetcy, bought the Mattersey estate for £20,000. This transaction produced a delightful example of Agnes's Marblehead gumption in a letter she sent to the estate trustees (Harry's friend William Wright and Thomas Pelham) in the spring of 1769.[110]

Sir Thomas claimed that she must pay him an additional £3,000 in settlement. With her annuity hanging in the balance, Agnes was not intimidated by Thomas's bullying. Demonstrating her detailed knowledge of the mortgages on Mattersey, she refused to pay a debt that no one— including Sir Harry—ever heard of and clearly states that she will not sign over the deed and close the sale until the trustees explain why she should:

> *Boston, NE March 6ʰ 1769*
> *I re'cd two letters last night from Sir Thos Frankland, which alarms and surprises me much…*
> *Sir Thos. says: "[The]…Mattersey Estate still is encumbered with £3000. To clear this and make a safe title Roger Talbot Esq. the attornies, Heirs Dame Agnes Frankland as Extr. To Sir Harry. [and] Sir Thomas Frankland only survivor Ex to his mother must join in some deed*

Agnes Surriage's signature. ©*The British Library Board Add.33088, f.332.*

> *or indenture to release the estate of this encumbrance. I have desired Mr. Pickering to draw up a proper one and we will forward it to you to execute."*

Agnes continues:

> *Sir Thomas observes in one of his letters that we all knew of £4000 being mortgaged upon the estates, but it is a very mysterious affair to me how the mortgage of £3000 can be, and if there is justly any such mortgage, why was it not produced before. I never heard poor Sir Harry say there was any such mortgage due but always said there was one of £4000, for which I know he only paid interest and for which the bankers can vouch; and it is very odd poor Sir Harry should not know of any such mortgage as £7000 was upon the Mattersey estate.*
>
> *…I must now beg the favor of you both will be so good as to examine into this affair, as I shall not sign a deed or whatever may be sent for that purpose till I have your and Col. Wright's advice.*

The solution of this discontinuity belongs to history. No one knows the contents of Pelham's reply to Agnes. Harry's brother did, however, take possession of Mattersey.

Alternating between Boston in the winter and Hopkinton in the summer, Lady Frankland enjoyed admiration and respect among the elite circles of Boston and Hopkinton.

But all of this was soon to change.

CHAPTER 24

"The Tories Lead a Devil of a Life"

—anonymous British soldier, 1774

In 1774, as tensions between the colonies and England began to mount, Agnes's presumed allegiance to the British government caused increasing suspicion of her loyalty.

She was living in Hopkinton when the war began at Lexington, only twenty miles away. The outbreak of open hostilities and a sense of personal danger were probably the strongest reasons for Agnes's decision to leave America quickly. Since Boston was under siege by militia, she would have to cross the rebel lines. Accordingly, she requested a pass from both the Committee of Safety and Dr. Joseph Warren, president of the Provincial Congress:

> HOPKINTON, May 15, 1775.
> Lady Frankland presents her compliments to the Committee of Safety, begs leave to acquaint them, that according to their request, she has sent in a list of things necessary for her intended voyage, which obtained Lady F. will esteem as a peculiar favour; and begs she may have her pass for Thursday.
> A list of things for Lady Frankland: Six trunks; one chest; three beds and bedding; six wethers; two pigs; one small keg of pickled tongues; some hay; three bags of corn.[111]

> HOPKINTON, May 15, 1775.
> Lady Frankland presents her compliments to Doctor Warren, begs leave to acquaint him, she has sent in a list of things necessary for her voyage to England; begs he would use his interest with the Committee of Safety,

The Brickpath (1727), Tory headquarters in Marblehead. *Photo by the author.*

that her request may be granted, which will lay Lady F. under a very great obligation to Doctor Warren, and on her return to New-England, if it is ever in her power, will return the obligation with thanks.

There is strong evidence that when she returned from Bath in 1768, Agnes had planned to live in Hopkinton and Boston for the rest of her life. She had every reason to stay: she owned both the Clark house and the Hopkinton estate. She was highly regarded in Boston. Her sister Mary and family, as well as her brother Isaac, were comfortably ensconced with her in Hopkinton.

But she must have believed the intensity of widespread hatred for the British government presented a genuine threat. Sheer desperation prompted her to take the extreme measure of concealing a gun, powder and ammunition in her chaise. She could never have imagined that Richard Devens,[112] one of Paul Revere's[113] cadre of British watchers, would learn of her hidden weapon.

A letter[114] dated May 18, 1775, from Richard Devens to John Thomas—a Kingston, Massachusetts physician and army officer in the French and Indian War—contained directions for "examining Lady Frankland, who has a pass to Boston from the Committee of Safety and who is supposed to have firearms with her effects."[115]

As a result, a man named Abner Craft halted and held Agnes and her party at the town line. From the *Journals of each Provincial congress of Massachusetts in 1774 and 1775*: "Notwithstanding the permission given by the Committee to Lady Frankland, to carry with her the articles of property mentioned in one of the resolves, some excitement arose among the inhabitants in the vicinity, from the preparations made for her departure. An armed party arrested her journey and detained her person and effects."

In their jingoistic passion, her neighbors ceased to see Agnes as the woman who grew up in a poor Marblehead fisherman's family, who attended their church, faithfully supported her siblings and was more than generous with her hospitality. She had become Lady Frankland, formerly the mistress—now widow—of a titled Englishman, and someone had seen her put a gun in her chaise. She was the enemy.

However, Abner's preemptive military act disturbed Dr. Warren and the civilian Provincial Congress:

> *Thursday, May 18, 1775—Resolved: That Mr. Abner Craft be, and is hereby directed forthwith to attend this congress. Mr. Craft accordingly attended and having heard the allegations against him, and having made his defense, withdrew. The congress then resolved that he should be gently admonished by the President, and be assured that the congress is determined to preserve their dignity and power over the military.*

After this parliamentary harrumph, the congress liberated Lady Frankland:

> *Resolved: That Lady Frankland be permitted to go into Boston with the following articles, viz: seven trunks, all the beds and furniture to them, all the boxes and crates, a basket of chickens and a bag of corn, two barrels and a hamper, two horses and two chaises, all the articles in the chaise excepting arms and ammunition[116]…which articles, having been examined by a committee, she is permitted to have them carried in without further examination.*

Then, to be sure that George Washington's army was protected from this dangerous woman, they appointed their own military escort: "Resolved: That Colonel Bond be and hereby is directed to appoint a guard of six men to escort Lady Frankland to Boston with such of her effects as this congress has permitted her to carry with her. And Colonel Bond is directed to wait on Colonel Thomas with a copy of the resolves of this congress respecting Lady Frankland."

One month after the shots were fired at Lexington common, armed minutemen arrested Agnes at Hopkinton. She and her entourage were searched, detained and then taken into Boston under armed guard. In every respect, Lady Frankland—like many others branded as Tories—was a casualty of war.

On June 17, 1775, only one month after her departure from Hopkinton, the Battle of Bunker Hill erupted practically in the backyard of Agnes's Garden Court Street home. She could not help but watch.

In *The Romance of New England Rooftrees*, Mary Caroline Crawford credits Agnes with dressing the wounds of British soldiers in her dining room. *The Loyalists of Massachusetts and the Other Side of the American Revolution*, by James Henry Stark, tells us she "took her part in relieving the sufferings of the British officers." However, I was not able to find a primary source to confirm that Agnes treated either British or American casualties.

Not long after Bunker Hill—there is no record of when—she sailed for England. As the Boston shoreline fell away, Lady Frankland probably had a good idea that she would never see her homeland again. That realization had to be a painful turning point in Agnes's life.

She was forty-nine years old, nearing the fifty-three-year life expectancy of an American woman in 1775. Since childhood, Agnes had been close to her family, especially her sister Mary. With the exception of Henry Cromwell, she was leaving all of her blood relations on the battleground of a land at war.

She had placed the Hopkinton estate under Mary's care, safe from confiscation by the Continental government.

Agnes, protégé of the Marblehead codfish widows, was now dependent on the kindness of Harry's British family and friends.

CHAPTER 25

Dame Agnes Frankland of Chichester

I couldn't help missing something in all of the official documents describing Agnes's tumultuous departure from Hopkinton. If a member of Lady Frankland's party had been an officer in the Royal Navy, would it not have created a stir somewhere along the chain of command, from the Provincial Congress, to the Committee of Safety to the Hopkinton militia? Yet there is no mention of Lieutenant Henry Cromwell, who was clearly living with Lady Frankland when he wrote to Thomas Pelham from Boston in November 1768.

In her monograph, *Dame Agnes Frankland*, Stella Palmer offered a possible answer. It is a quote from the register of All Saints Church in Chichester: "Baptism. 1775, 3ʳᵈ April. Cromwell Cato, a negro Boy of Lady Frankland from Boston in America."[117]

Slavery had been illegal in England since 1772, but it was the custom for emancipated slaves to take the names of their former owners. Palmer uses this record to establish that Henry Cromwell was living in Chichester at the time.

The mention of Lady Frankland is interesting. At the time of Cato Cromwell's baptism, Agnes was in Hopkinton preparing to leave. It is possible that someone else—most likely Henry—had previously taken either Cato's pregnant mother or the newly born infant from Boston to Chichester. If Palmer's conclusion is correct, Henry Cromwell left Boston and took up residence in Chichester sometime between 1768 and 1775.[118] It was a logical place for Henry to settle. He would be close to Portsmouth, the Royal Navy's

Number 5 West Pallant, Chichester, UK, the home of Dame Agnes Frankland. *Photo by Anne Scicluna.*

most important dockyard in the late eighteenth century. Chichester was near the home of that Frankland family benefactor, Thomas Pelham, who had recently succeeded his cousin Thomas Pelham Howles (the Duke of Newcastle) as second Baron Pelham of Stamner. In addition, Reverend John Frankland, Sir Harry's first cousin, was a prominent Chichester clergyman.[119]

Agnes went straight to Chichester from Boston and stayed with her cousin John and his wife Mary after arriving in England during the summer of 1775. Two years later, she had her own home at 5 West Pallant[120] in the center of town.

The following quote is from a letter, dated July 15, 1778, written by Frederic Robinson to his brother, the British ambassador at Madrid. In it, he gives a euphemistic hint of Agnes's problems with her American properties: "Lady Frankland and Mrs. Ventham dined on Monday. Latter engaged to marry Mr. Cromwell, now at sea. Lady Frankland currently receiving nothing from her American estate due to the troubles."

Henry Cromwell married Mary Ventham, a widow, on January 2, 1779. By 1783, he had a son and a daughter, in addition to a stepdaughter. The

Priory Park in Chichester, showing (right) the remains of Bailey castle, (center) Greyfriars chancel and (background) Chichester Cathedral. *Photo by Anne Scicluna.*

Cromwell home was situated a quarter of a mile to the north of Agnes's, so she undoubtedly enjoyed much time with her grandchildren.

On October 25, 1781, Lady Agnes Frankland married John Drew, a widower, the bailiff of Chichester. She moved into John's house with his seventeen-year-old son.[121]

It was not to last. On April 23, 1783, Agnes died of "an inflammation on the lungs." She was fifty-seven years old. She is buried at St. Pancras in the Drew family vault, which lies at the northeast corner of Chichester—four thousand miles from Marblehead. Her plaque reads:

> *Dame Agnes Frankland*
> *Relict of Sir Charles Henry Frankland, Bart.*
> *and late wife of John Drew*
> *Died April 23, 1783*

The Real Agnes Surriage

Uncovering the real story of Agnes Surriage began as a hobby; it quickly became an obsession and wound up as a mission. Living on the spot that marks the most pivotal moment in her life absolutely influenced the dynamics of my relationship with this time-distant person. Participating in Marblehead's colonial past as a historical interpreter while being immersed in the town's powerful ambience gave my study of Agnes and Harry a depth beyond anything I would have been able to achieve in a different venue.

At some point, Agnes became a part of my experience in the present rather than a disembodied woman from the past. I am not suggesting anything supernatural. It was more like a contextualization of my work. Whether I was approaching a library table to take notes from a reference book, sitting at the computer writing or performing research on the Internet, my intensity was heightened by anticipation of a visit with an old friend. This is nothing unusual. Every writer identifies with his or her characters, real or fictional. But my identification involved more than reliving Agnes's experiences. I felt that I was watching her life unfold in real time.

Agnes Surriage performed many roles during her transformation from Marblehead's fourteen-year-old servant girl to Chichester's Dame Agnes Frankland:

1726–1740: Fourteen years of near invisibility as a fisherman's daughter living among the codfish widows of Marblehead.

1740–42: Thrust into maturity by an unexpected pregnancy.

1741–1752: Separated from her baby, she experienced eleven years of exposure in a bewildering new environment where she met with condescension and finally contempt and humiliation.

1752–1754: A brief two-year respite in Hopkinton as the mistress of a gentrified bureaucrat.

1754–55: Ostracized by the Frankland family in England and secretly married in Portugal.

November 1, 1755: Survived the natural disaster of the century.

1755–1768: Followed by thirteen years as Lady Agnes Frankland, the wife of a foreign diplomat traveling between England, Boston, Hopkinton and Portugal.

1768–1783: And finally, fifteen years as the dowager Lady Frankland, driven from her homeland and deprived of her property.

The Agnes Surriage I found was a quiet woman, gentle and kind yet in no way supplicant or timid. Her Marblehead heritage served her well. Lady Frankland lived to command the respect of the very people who had scorned her low birth and premarital relationship with Frankland. To the end, she was stalwart in adversity and resourceful under pressure.

Henry Cromwell

I n November 1781, Henry Cromwell was promoted to captain and placed in command of HMS *Victory*.[122] On December 2, 1781, he joined eleven other ships of the line and five frigates to intercept a French convoy, which sailed from Brest on December 10. Neither Henry nor his commanding officer, Admiral Kempenfelt, knew that the convoy was escorted by twenty-one French ships of the line.

Kempenfelt ordered a chase when the French were sighted on December 12. The British fleet was able to capture fifteen convoy ships before nature saved them from certain destruction: the French escort was dispersed in a gale and forced to return home. This action is recorded in naval history as the Second Battle of Ushant.

Cromwell became a rear admiral in January 1801 and a vice admiral in July 1810.

Was Henry Cromwell an admiral in name only? Nason and others claim that he retired from the service before the end of the American Revolution because he was unwilling to fight against his "native country." The only hint that this might be true came from Curatorial Officer Iain MacKenzie of the Royal Navy's History Branch:[123]

> *It is a little surprising that, given his rank and date of death, he doesn't appear in any of the contemporary biographical dictionaries, nor does he even get an obituary notice in the* Naval Chronicle, *the Navy's "in house" magazine of the time. This, and his absence from the naval histories of the French Revolutionary and Napoleonic Wars, tends to confirm that he*

*was not in active service, but rather what was called a "Yellow Admiral,"
one who never hoisted his flag in active command.*

But a singularly more auspicious event in Henry Cromwell's life quickly eclipsed his naval career.

Sir Harry's younger brother William quit his peripatetic life in the Middle East and returned to England during the latter half of the eighteenth century. In 1768, he bought Muntham Court, a luxurious mansion situated on two thousand acres in the West Sussex town of Findon.

Soon after he arrived, Frankland began turning Muntham Court into an industrial museum. According to historian Valorie Martin, "His intention in life appears to have been 'to collect and employ every newly-invented machine.'" In addition, he became famous for devices of his own construction, which included an organ, machines for weaving and bookbinding, a water mill, an air pump and a metronome.

Since Findon was a scant sixteen miles north of Chichester, the home of Henry Cromwell and his wife, Mary, it is logical to assume that William Frankland connected with his nephew at some point in time.

Frankland was obsessed with his lineage, especially the fact that he was descended from Oliver Cromwell. Sometime in the late 1770s, he commissioned the American painter Mather Brown to do portraits depicting his genealogy.[124] Brown painted the entire descending line, five portraits in all: Oliver Cromwell, Frances Cromwell, Elizabeth Frankland, Henry Frankland and William Frankland, the wizard of Muntham Court himself.

William Frankland never married. He died on December 28, 1805, leaving in his will a surprise worthy of his lifelong eccentricity: he bequeathed Muntham Court, in entirety, to Admiral Henry Cromwell—with the proviso that Henry and all of his descendants change their surname to Frankland and adopt the Frankland coat of arms.

In the end, William Frankland left Henry a proposition he could not refuse. Muntham was a treasure well beyond the reach of a retired naval officer. But he also left a fascinating enigma for posterity. Was this the beneficent gesture of a childless uncle for his favorite nephew? Or was it the final manipulation of a proud man who could not bear the thought of his precious Cromwell lineage being tarnished by the bloodline of a brother's natural son? It is interesting that his change of name would give Henry the same surname as his father and the woman I strongly believe to be his mother.

Wasting no time, Admiral Henry Cromwell became Admiral Henry Frankland in the first week of February 1806. He died in 1814. At his request, he is buried in Chichester, near Agnes's tomb.

Notes

Introduction

1. Peterson, *Marblehead Myths*.
2. McCullough, *John Adams*, 104.

Chapter 1

3. Noyes, Libby and Davis, *Dictionary of Maine and New Hampshire*, 115.
4. Ibid.
5. Second Church Records, Marblehead Museum and Historical Society.
6. Ibid.
7. On September 25 of the same year, Holyoke, who had already lost two daughters and his first wife, wrote in the baptismal record: "Margaret Holyoke infant of Edward and Margaret Holyoke." And in the margin: "My own child." Second Church Records, Marblehead Museum and Historical Society.
8. The town house would not be built until 1728.
9. Ahead of her were Edward; Mary, baptized January 14, 1722; and Josiah, April 5, 1725. She was followed by Thomas, May 5, 1728; John, June 28, 1730; Hugh, September 17, 1732; and Isaac, who is somewhat of an enigma. He is listed in Marblehead Vital Records without a date of birth or baptism.
10. Heyrman, *Commerce and Culture*, 217.

11. Ibid.

12. Ibid., 257.

13. Ibid., 248.

14. The U.S. infant mortality rate was 6.7 percent in 2008.

15. Roads, *History and Traditions*, 49.

16. It is interesting to note that Reverend Edward Holyoke, liberal pastor of Marblehead Second Church, was not only inoculated but also spent the duration of the epidemic in Boston.

17. Heyrman, *Commerce and Culture*, 308.

18. Roads, *History and Traditions*, 49.

19. Noyes, Libby and Davis, *Genealogical Dictionary of Maine and New Hampshire*, 554.

CHAPTER 2

20. Wild, *East India Company*.

21. Ibid., 63.

22. en.wikipedia.org/wiki/British_East_India_Company.

23. *Complete Baronage*.

24. www.findonvillage.com/0300_william_frankland_arrives_in_findon.htm.

25. Levin, *Abigail Adams*, 151.

CHAPTER 3

26. Roads, *History and Traditions*.

27. Swett, *Swett Family*.

28. Heyrman, *Commerce and Culture*, 237–41.

CHAPTER 4

29. Wild, *East India Company*, 64.

30. Nottinghamshire Archives, 925/18.

31. Wilson, *Old Fort William*, 118.

32. The jaw-breaking official name of the British East India Company

33. The British Library, IOR/H/68.

34. Wilson, *Old Fort William*.

35. Ibid.

CHAPTER 5

36. Venn, *Alumni Cantabrigienses*.
37. *Peerage and Baronetage*, en.wikipedia.org/wiki/Wikipedia:WikiProject_Peerage_and_Baronetage. It did not hurt matters that his namesake, Sir Thomas Frankland, was on the Admiralty Board.
38. Lieutenant Colonel Charles Russell with the British army in Prussia.
39. *Report on the Manuscripts of Mrs. Frankland-Russell-Astley* (London: Mackie & Co. Ltd., 1900). Historical Manuscripts Commission. Printed for Her Majesty's Stationery Office by Mackie & Co. Ltd.
40. Fortunately, I did not have to go to England to get them. The British government has made a treasure-trove of archives available at www.a2a.org.uk/default.asp.
41. This refers to Harry, not his father. I found many references to "Heny Frankland, esq." dated after 1728, when the governor of Fort William died.

CHAPTER 6

42. A two-masted square-rigged ship similar to a brig, fitted with a small third mast at the stern, which carried a triangular sail called a "spanker."
43. This remarkable document, which resides in the Marblehead Museum and Historical Society library, is the first autobiography written by a New England fisherman. It is filled with Bowen's distinctive watercolor sketches.
44. Smith, *Slavery, Family and Gentry Capitalism*, 122.
45. Ibid., 100.

CHAPTER 7

46. Not withstanding his generosity to the town, Gale is also known as one of the witnesses who testified against Wilmot Redd, the only woman from Marblehead to be hanged during the Salem witch trials of 1692.
47. Bodnar, *Remaking America*.
48. "Historical Markers Erected by the Massachusetts Bay Colony Tercentenary Commission" Samuel Elliot Morrison, State of Massachusetts, 1930.

CHAPTER 8

49. For this chapter, I am indebted to the Marblehead Museum and Historical Society's publication, "The Fountain Inn: Agnes Surriage and Sir Harry Frankland," first delivered by Nathan P. Sanborn as a lecture before the Marblehead Historical Society on December 8, 1904, and the *Essex Antiquarian* 2, no. 8 (August 1898).
50. Essex Registry of Deeds, Book 39, leaf 15.
51. Sanborn, "Fountain Inn," 12.
52. Dow and Edmonds, *Pirates of the New England Coast.*
53. Roads, *History and Traditions,* 52.

CHAPTER 9

54. Platt, *Smuggling in the British Isles.*
55. From the Phillips Library, Peabody Essex Museum, Salem, MA.
56. McClellan, *Smuggling in the American Colonies,* 5, 29, 36, 41.
57. Demos, *Remarkable Providences,* 191–209.

CHAPTER 10

58. Atkins, *Sex in Literature.*
59. Ibid.
60. Barker-Benfield, *Culture of Sensibility.*
61. Godbeeer, *Sexual Revolution in Early America.*
62. Ibid., 239.
63. Knoll, *America's God.*
64. Heyrman, *Commerce and Culture,* 367.
65. Ibid., 377.
66. Doyle, *The Colonies.*
67. Franklin, *Autobiography.*
68. Palmer, *Dame Agnes Frankland.*

CHAPTER 11

69. Quote from an account of their meeting in *The Dictionary of American Biography.*

CHAPTER 12

70. Nason, *Sir Charles Henry Frankland*, 42.
71. Bynner, *Agnes Surriage*.
72. Quiller-Couch, *Lady Good-for-Nothing*, 5.
73. *Complete Baronage*, Volume III William Pollard & Company, Exeter.
74. From notes in Payne-Gallwey's handwriting at the Massachusetts Historical Society.
75. I wrote to the Yorkshire Archaeological Society, and it sent me a photocopy for verification.
76. The journal is the property of the Massachusetts Historical Society.

CHAPTER 13

77. He was not Sir Harry in 1742. He did not receive the baronetcy until the death of his Uncle Thomas in 1747.
78. Holyoke became president of Harvard in 1738. He was replaced by Simon Bradstreet.
79. The accepted euphemism of the time was "natural son."
80. Lincoln, *Correspondence of William Shirley*.
81. Ibid.
82. Bacon, *Literary Pilgrimages*.
83. Roads, *History and Traditions*, 44.
84. Seybolt, *Private Schools*.

CHAPTER 14

85. *Complete Baronage*.
86. Deeds of the Berkswell Hall Estate (CR2440). © Warwickshire County Record Office.

CHAPTER 15

87. This refers to British merchants engaging in West Indies trade, once again emphasizing their reliance on the sugar plantations.
88. Updike, *Memoirs of the Rhode Island Bar*.

89. Nason, *Sir Charles Henry Frankland*.
90. Boucé, *Sexuality in Eighteenth-Century Britain*, 10.

CHAPTER 16

91. Annals of the King's Chapel, www.archive.org/details/annalsofkingscha01foot.
92. Records of the Society for the Propagation of the Gospel in Foreign Parts, Collection 155, www.wheaton.edu/bgc/archives/GUIDES/155.htm.
93. The description of Harry Frankland's Hopkinton estate is from "Recollections of Frankland Farm," a narrative by Elias Nason, who lived in the original mansion from 1842 to 1846. It is on file in the Hopkinton Public Library.
94. "Mr. Clflin" quoted by Frederick J. Stimson, *New York Times*, December 3, 1910.
95. A project of the WPA.

CHAPTER 17

96. Public Records Office, London.
97. The letter is not dated, but he mentions inaccuracies in Nason, Byner and Quiller-Couch, the latter book published in 1910.

CHAPTER 19

98. From the Archives of Syon Abbey, Marley Head, South Brent, Devon.
99. Mr. Wolfall, Surgeon, to James Parsons, MD. FRS.
100. Kendrick, *Lisbon Earthquake*.
101. www.fordham.edu/halsall/mod/1755lisbonearthquake.html.
102. www.bbc.co.uk/dna/h2g2/A2309276.
103. Kendrick, *Lisbon Earthquake*.

Chapter 20

104. Ibid.
105. En route from Belem back to England.
106. Kendrick cites the reported case of a fifteen-year-old girl who had been trapped clutching an image of St. Anthony being found safe and unharmed.

Chapter 22

107. Missouri–Columbia University Libraries.
108. Today, it is a town square called Terreiro Salgado, the "Salty Ground."

Chapter 23

109. Pelham Papers, British Museum.
110. Ibid.

Chapter 24

111. DeFronsac, *Rise of the United Empire Loyalists*, 94.
112. "I was informed by Richard Devens Esq. that he met that evening, after sunset, nine officers of the ministerial army, mounted on good horses, and armed, going towards Concord." "Paul Revere's Account of His Midnight Ride to Lexington," ahp.gatech.edu/midnight_ride_1775.html.
113. Revere knew Lady Frankland well. She was his neighbor.
114. Richard Frothingham Papers, 1683–1865, Massachusetts Historical Society.
115. Reel 3 171.1.7.30 Resolves of Massachusetts Provincial, ahp.gatech.edu/midnight_ride_1775.html.
116. "One gun, one sword, and one small flask with a small quantity of powder and lead."

CHAPTER 25

117. Cato's burial is recorded on April 12, 1776.
118. Nason, in my opinion, makes an unfounded assumption when he says, "Attended by Henry Cromwell, she soon after sailed for England," a statement for which he gives no source. Nason, *Sir Charles Henry Frankland*, 104.
119. Prebendary of Bracklesham and Canon Residentiary of Chichester Cathedral, a statement for which he gives no source.
120. The building subsequently became the town post office.
121. Chichester Papers, No. 41, a statement for which he gives no source.

EPILOGUE

122. Built in the 1760s, *Victory* is the oldest warship in the world still under commission. It became famous as Admiral Nelson's flagship in the 1805 Battle of Trafalgar and today rests in No. 2 Dry Dock at Portsmouth's Royal Naval Dockyard.
123. Letter to the author, March 2, 2010.
124. www.findonvillage.com.

Bibliography

Atkins, John. *Sex in Literature*. Vol. 4, *High Noon: The Seventeenth and Eighteenth Centuries*. London: John Calder, Riverrun Press, 1982.

Bacon, Edwin Monroe. *Literary Pilgrimages in New England*. Vol. 2. N.p.: Silver Burdett & Co., 1902.

Barker-Benfield, G.J. *The Culture of Sensibility: Sex and Sensibility in Eighteenth-Century Britain*. Chicago: University of Chicago Press, 1992.

Barker, Hannah, and Elaine Chalus, ed. *Gender in Eighteenth-Century England: Roles, Representations and Responsibilities*. New York: Addison Wesley Longman, Ltd., 1997.

Bodnar, John E. *Remaking America: Public Memory, Commemoration, and Patriotism in the Twentieth Century*. Princeton, NJ: Princeton University Press, 1992.

Boucé, Paul Gabriel, ed. *Sexuality in Eighteenth-Century Britain*. Manchester, UK: Manchester University Press, 1982.

Bynner, Edwin Lassetter. *Agnes Surriage*. Boston: Houghton Mifflin & Company, 1898.

Complete Baronage. Vol. 3. Exeter, UK: William Pollard & Co. Ltd., 1902.

DeFronsac, Viscount. *Rise of the United Empire Loyalists.* Kingston, ON: British Whig Publishing Co. Ltd., 1906.

Demos, John. *Remarkable Providences, Readings on Early American History: Autobiography of the Reverend John Barnard.* Boston: Northeastern University Press, 1972.

Dow, George Francis, and John Henry Edmonds. *The Pirates of the New England Coast.* Salem, MA: Marine Research Society, 1923.

Doyle, J.A. *The Colonies under the House of Hanover.* London: Longmans, Green and Co., 1907.

Franklin, Benjamin. *The Autobiography of Benjamin Franklin.* Boston: Houghton Mifflin & Company, 1923.

French, Allen. *The First Year of the American Revolution.* Boston: Houghton Mifflin & Company, 1934.

Godbeer, Richard. *Sexual Revolution in Early America.* Baltimore, MD: Johns Hopkins University Press, 2004.

Heyrman, Christine Leigh. *Commerce and Culture: The Maritime Communities of Colonial Massachusetts, 1690–1750.* New York: W.W. Norton & Co., 1984.

Holmes, Oliver Wendell. "Agnes, a Ballad." www.readbookonline.net/readOnLine/6848.

Kendrick, T.D. *The Lisbon Earthquake.* Philadelphia: J.B. Lippincott Co., 1955.

Ketchum, Richard M. *The Battle for Bunker Hill.* New York: Doubleday Books, 1974.

Knoll, Mark. *America's God: From Jonathan Edwards to Abraham Lincoln.* Oxford, UK: Oxford University Press, n.d.

Levin, Phyllis Lee. *Abigail Adams: A Biography.* New York: St. Martin's Griffin/Thomas Dunne Books, 2001.

Lincoln, Charles Henry, PhD. *Correspondence of William Shirley*. New York: MacMillan & Co., 1912.

Mackay, Ruddock F. *Admiral Hawke*. Oxford, UK: Clarendon Press, 1965.

McClellan, William S. *Smuggling in the American Colonies at the Outbreak of the Revolution with Special Reference to the West Indies Trade*. New York: Moffat, Yard and Company, 1912.

McCullough, David. *John Adams*. New York: Simon & Schuster, 2001.

Nason, M.A., Elias. *Sir Charles Henry Frankland, Baronet: or, Boston in the Colonial Times*. Albany, NY: J. Munsell, 1865.

Noyes, Sybil, C.T. Libby and W.G. Davis. *Genealogical Dictionary of Maine and New Hampshire*. Portland, ME: 1928–1939.

Old North Church. *Under the Golden Cod: A Shared History of the Old North Church and the Town of Marblehead, Massachusetts*. Canaan, NH: Phoenix Press, First Church of Christ in Marblehead, 1984.

Palmer, Stella. *Dame Agnes Frankland, 1726–1783, and Some Chichester Contemporaries*. Chichester, UK: Chichester City Council, 1964.

Peterson, Pam. *Marblehead Myths, Legends and Lore*. Charleston, SC: The History Press, 2007.

Platt, Richard. *Smuggling in the British Isles: A History*. London: Tempus Publishing Ltd., 2010.

Quiller-Couch, A.T. ("Q"). *Lady Good-for-Nothing: A Man's Portrait of a Woman*. New York: Charles Scribner's Sons, 1910.

Roads, Samuel, Jr. *History and Traditions of Marblehead*. Boston: Houghton Mifflin & Company, 1881.

Sanborn, Nathan P. "The Fountain Inn: Agnes Surriage and Sir Harry Frankland." A paper read before the Marblehead Historical Society, December 9, 1904. Published by the society, 1921.

Seybolt, Robert Francis. *The Private Schools of Colonial Boston*. Cambridge, MA: Harvard University Press, 1935.

Smith, S.D. *Slavery, Family, and Gentry Capitalism in the British Atlantic: The World of the Lascelles, 1648–1834*. Cambridge, UK: Cambridge University Press, 2006.

Swett, Colonel Ben H., USAF (Retired). *The Swett Family of Marblehead*. swett-genealogy.com.

Thompson, Roger. *Sex in Middlesex: Popular Mores in a Massachusetts County, 1649–1699*. Amherst: University of Massachusetts Press, 1986.

Updike, Wilkins, Esq. *Memoirs of the Rhode Island Bar*. Boston: Thomas H. Webb, 1842.

Venn, J.A. *Alumni Cantabrigienses: A Biographical List of All Known Students, Graduates and Holders of Office at the University of Cambridge*. Cambridge, UK: University Press, 1900.

Vickery, Amanda. *The Gentleman's Daughter: Women's Lives in Georgian England*. New Haven, CT: Yale University Press, 1998.

Wild, Antony. *The East India Company*. New York: HarperCollins, n.d.

Wilson, C.R., ed. *Old Fort William in Bengal: A Selection of Official Documents Dealing with Its History*. London: published for the Government of India, John Murray, 1906.